Bloom's

GUIDES

Arthur Miller's
The Crucible
New Edition

Adventures of Huckleberry Finn
All the Pretty Horses
Animal Farm
The Autobiography of Malcolm X
The Awakening
The Bell Jar
Beloved
Beowulf
Black Boy
The Bluest Eye
Brave New World
The Canterbury Tales
Catch-22
The Catcher in the Rye
The Chosen
The Crucible
Cry, the Beloved Country
Death of a Salesman
Fahrenheit 451
A Farewell to Arms
Frankenstein
The Glass Menagerie
The Grapes of Wrath
Great Expectations
The Great Gatsby
Hamlet
The Handmaid's Tale
Heart of Darkness
The House on Mango Street
I Know Why the Caged Bird Sings
The Iliad
Invisible Man
Jane Eyre

The Joy Luck Club
The Kite Runner
Lord of the Flies
Macbeth
Maggie: A Girl of the Streets
The Member of the Wedding
The Metamorphosis
Native Son
Night
1984
The Odyssey
Oedipus Rex
Of Mice and Men
One Hundred Years of Solitude
Pride and Prejudice
Ragtime
A Raisin in the Sun
The Red Badge of Courage
Romeo and Juliet
The Scarlet Letter
A Separate Peace
Slaughterhouse-Five
Snow Falling on Cedars
The Stranger
A Streetcar Named Desire
The Sun Also Rises
A Tale of Two Cities
Their Eyes Were Watching God
The Things They Carried
To Kill a Mockingbird
Uncle Tom's Cabin
The Waste Land
Wuthering Heights

Bloom's
GUIDES

Arthur Miller's
The Crucible
New Edition

Edited & with an Introduction
by Harold Bloom

BLOOM'S
LITERARY CRITICISM
An imprint of Infobase Publishing

Bloom's Guides: The Crucible—New Edition
Copyright © 2010 by Infobase Publishing
Introduction © 2010 by Harold Bloom

All rights reserved. No part of this book may be reproduced or utilized in any form or by any means, electronic or mechanical, including photocopying, recording, or by any information storage or retrieval systems, without permission in writing from the publisher. For information contact:

Bloom's Literary Criticism
An imprint of Infobase Publishing
132 West 31st Street
New York NY 10001

Library of Congress Cataloging-in-Publication Data
Arthur Miller's The crucible / edited and with an introduction by Harold Bloom. — New ed.
    p. cm. — (Bloom's guides)
    Includes bibliographical references and index.
    ISBN 978-1-60413-815-3 (acid-free paper)   1. Miller, Arthur, 1915–2005. Crucible.   2. Witchcraft in literature.   3. Trials (Witchcraft) in literature.   4. Salem (Mass.)—In literature.   I. Bloom, Harold.   II. Title: Crucible.
    PS3525.I5156C7377 2010
    812'.52—dc22   2010001312

Bloom's Literary Criticism books are available at special discounts when purchased in bulk quantities for businesses, associations, institutions, or sales promotions. Please call our Special Sales Department in New York at (212) 967–8800 or (800) 322–8755.

You can find Bloom's Literary Criticism on the World Wide Web at
http://www.chelseahouse.com

Contributing editor: Portia Williams Weiskel
Cover designed by Takeshi Takahashi
Composition by IBT Global, Troy NY
Cover printed by Yurchak Printing, Landisville, PA
Book printed and bound by Yurchak Printing, Landisville, PA
Date printed: November, 2011
Printed in the United States of America
This book is printed on acid-free paper.

All links and Web addresses were checked and verified to be correct at the time of publication. Because of the dynamic nature of the Web, some addresses and links may have changed since publication and may no longer be valid.

Contents

Introduction

HAROLD BLOOM

More than 50 years ago, in his introduction to his *Collected Plays*, Arthur Miller meditated on *The Crucible*, staged four years before, in 1953. A year after that first production, Miller was refused a passport, and in 1956–57 he endured the active persecution of the American witch hunt for suspected communists. The terror created in some of his former friends and associates by the possibility of being branded warlocks and witches "underlies every word in *The Crucible*," according to Miller. "Every word" necessarily is hyperbolical, since *The Crucible* attempts to be a personal tragedy as well as a social drama. Miller, Ibsen's disciple, nevertheless suffers an anxiety of influence in *The Crucible* not so much in regard to Ibsen's *An Enemy of the People* but in relation to George Bernard Shaw's *Saint Joan*. The frequent echoes of *Saint Joan* seem involuntary and are distracting and perhaps fatal to the aesthetic value of *The Crucible*. For all its moral earnestness, *Saint Joan* is enhanced by the Shavian ironic wit, a literary quality totally absent from Miller, here and elsewhere. Though a very well-made play, *The Crucible* rarely escapes a certain dreariness in performance and does not gain by rereading.

This is not to deny the humane purpose nor the theatrical effectiveness of *The Crucible* but only to indicate a general limitation, here and elsewhere, in Miller's dramatic art. Eric Bentley has argued shrewdly that "one never knows what a Miller play is about: politics or sex." Is *The Crucible* a personal tragedy, founded on Proctor's sexual infidelity, or is it a play of social protest and warning? There is no reason it should not be both, except for Miller's inability to fuse the genres. Here he falls short of his master, Ibsen, who concealed Shakespearean tragic purposes within frameworks of social issues yet invariably unified the two modes. Still, one can be grateful that Miller has not revised *The Crucible* on the basis of his own afterthoughts, which have emphasized the absolute evil of the Salem powers, Danforth and Hathorne. These worthies already are mere facades, opaque to Miller's understanding and our own. Whatever their religious sensibility may or may not have been, Miller has no imaginative understanding of it, and we therefore confront them only as puppets. Had Miller made them even more malevolent, our bafflement would have been even greater. I am aware that I tend to be an uncompromising aesthete, and I cannot dissent from the proven theatrical effectiveness of *The Crucible*. Its social benignity is also beyond my questioning; American society continues to benefit by this play. We would have to mature beyond our national tendency to moral and religious self-righteousness for *The Crucible* to dwindle into another period piece, and that maturation is nowhere in sight.

Biographical Sketch

Born in Manhattan on October 17, 1915, Arthur Miller was the second child of three for Isadore and Augusta Miller, a well-to-do Jewish couple. In 1929 the stock market crash and Depression forced Arthur Miller's father out of the coat business and their family out of their home to a small frame house in Brooklyn. Upon graduating from Abraham Lincoln High School in 1932, Miller started saving as much as he could from his income at an auto-parts warehouse so he could go to college. He occasionally would read on the subway on his way to work, and when he happened upon Dostoevsky's *The Brothers Karamazov*, Miller "all at once believed [he] was born to be a writer."

But when he applied to the University of Michigan, Miller was turned down until he tried for a third time with a convincing letter he sent to the admissions officer. Having heard the school gave writing prizes, he enrolled in journalism classes, and within eighteen months he began writing plays, winning the Avery Hopwood Award on his first try for a piece he had written in just four days, *Honors at Dawn*. He received another Hopwood for his second work, *No Villain*, just one year later in 1937.

After he received his B.A. in 1938, Miller went back to New York and worked with the Federal Theatre Project until it was abolished; he then found himself on welfare. He completed his play, *The Golden Years*, and to make money he wrote numerous radio scripts—work he hated. In 1940 Miller married Mary Grace Slattery, to whom he had become engaged at the University of Michigan; they moved to Brooklyn and eventually had two children. He held various odd jobs and kept writing for the next four years, while she served as the main breadwinner, working as a waitress and editor.

In 1944 Miller had his first Broadway production. The play's title, *The Man Who Had All the Luck*, certainly was not applicable to Miller at the time, for the piece struggled through only six performances, although it managed to win the Theatre Guild National Award. A back injury kept Miller out of the military, but he visited army camps during the war and published his journal, *Situation Normal*, in 1944. By 1945 Miller switched gears and wrote a novel, *Focus*, about anti-Semitism. He became increasingly involved in leftist organizations and liberal causes. Then in 1947 his first son was born, and his first successful Broadway play was produced, *All My Sons*. It showed the after-effects of World War II on a family whose father had sold faulty plane parts to the government.

But Miller's most famous play by far is *Death of a Salesman*, which centers on a dejected salesman's final days. It was composed in six weeks on a typewriter Miller had bought with the money he earned from his first Hopwood. That year—1949—the Pulitzer Prize was awarded to Miller for the first time. He also received the New York Drama Critics' Circle Award for the work, which ran through 1950 for 742 performances. The same year Miller traveled to California to work on a film project. There he met Marilyn Monroe, and they saw each other frequently for many weeks.

In 1951 Miller published an adaptation of Henrik Ibsen's *An Enemy of the People*. Political commitments took up much of Miller's time then, and in 1953 he put his warnings about the dangers of mass hysteria and government power into the form of *The Crucible*, a work about the Salem witch trials that was readily construed as a metaphor for the McCarthy hearings then taking place. By 1955 Miller's marriage was falling apart, and he met Monroe again at a theater party. They were seen together more often, and after his divorce, Miller married Monroe in 1956.

The Crucible was well-received, but it helped bring Miller negative attention of another sort. In June 1956 he was subpoenaed to appear before the House Un-American Activities Committee. Curiously, in the midst of his political troubles, he announced that he and Monroe had been secretly married. Before the committee, Miller freely admitted his past associations with leftist groups, stating they had ended in

1950. Refusing to be a "good citizen" who would identify other communists, he named not one.

During this time, in 1955, Miller saw his *A View from the Bridge* produced on a double bill with a short play, *A Memory of Two Mondays*. He also won his second Pulitzer Prize. His screenplay for the 1961 film *The Misfits* was created for his wife, who starred in it with Clark Gable, but shortly thereafter in that same year, they were divorced. Also in that year, Miller's mother died at the age of eighty.

In 1962 Miller married the photographer Inge Morath, with whom he had two children and collaborated on several books, writing text to accompany her images. By 1964, Miller's *After the Fall* was produced, creating more controversy than any of his previous work. Many critics balked at what they construed to be an excessively autobiographical piece.

Miller covered the Nazi trials in Frankfurt for the *New York Herald Tribune* and then wrote *Incident at Vichy* (1965), a short play about Nazism and anti-Semitism in Vichy, France. In the same year he traveled extensively in Europe to oversee productions of his various works.

In 1966 approximately seventeen million viewers saw *Death of a Saleman* on television, twenty times the number who had seen the play when it was on Broadway. A collection of short stories, *I Don't Need You Anymore* (1967), followed, as did another play, *The Price* (1968). He was a member of the Connecticut delegation to the fateful Democratic National Convention in 1972, and he continued to be politically active and voice his beliefs. In 1973 the comic *The Creation of the World and Other Business* was produced. They were followed by *The Archbishop's Ceiling* (1977) and *The American Clock* (1980).

In 1983 Miller directed *Death of a Salesman* in China. In 1984 *Up from Paradise* was published, followed by *Danger: Memory!* in 1986, and his autobiography, *Timebends: A Life*, in 1987. He continued to see his works published and produced not only in theater but also on television. In 1994 *Broken Glass* was published, and in 1995 production began on a film version of *The Crucible*. A collection of his essays was published in 2000, and in 2002 his play *Resurrection Blues* was produced.

Miller died in 2005. Dustin Hoffman, one of the most famous Willy Lomans, described Miller in *Arthur Miller and Company* as "so articulate. He's this great storyteller. He sounds like this New York cab driver; he's so unpretentious and earthy. You're laughing one minute, then you're thinking the next, and touched the next."

The Story Behind the Story

When *The Crucible* was published and produced in 1953, many audiences and critics felt that the play, with a plot focused on the Salem witch trials of the late 1600s, was an analogy for the McCarthy investigations that were going on at the time. Some of the same issues, such as mass hysteria and unchecked power, were at the forefront of both historical events.

In the 1950s, the U.S. House of Representatives' Un-American Activities Committee questioned people suspected of being communists. The committee interviewed individuals about their activities and also asked them for names of other suspected communists. Many were blacklisted, fired from their jobs, and would not be hired elsewhere. Miller cites the extreme case of a man who was fired because he explained that he had no connections with leftists and had nothing he could give the court, namely a confession; as a result of the trauma, the man could not summon the strength to leave his home for more than a year. Miller himself was subpoenaed a few years after *The Crucible* was produced and testified that his associations with leftist groups had ended in 1950. He would not supply names of others he knew to have such associations at that time or in the past, voicing his belief against such an action in nearly the same words used by a character in his own play.

The events of the 1950s disturbed Miller, as he would later describe in his introduction to his *Collected Plays*, which was published in 1957:

> It was not only the rise of "McCarthyism" that moved me, but something which seemed much more weird and mysterious. It was the fact that a political, objective, knowledgeable campaign from the far Right was capable of creating not only a terror, but a new subjective reality. . . . The wonder of it all struck me that so practical and picayune a cause, carried forward by such manifestly ridiculous men, should be capable of paralyzing thought

itself, and worse, causing to billow up such persuasive clouds of "mysterious" feelings within people. . . .

With this in mind, Miller turned to the Salem witch trials, events he had similarly thought were nearly incomprehensible. He did extensive research on these trials using, among other things, various public records in Salem. Miller realized this was the right venue for his new play when he discovered one piece of information, namely that Abigail, the leader of the hysterical girls who appeared in court, had accused Elizabeth Proctor of being a witch but had not accused Elizabeth's husband, John. Miller changed historical events here slightly when he wrote his play, in that he raised Abigail's age and lowered John Proctor's to make an affair between them believable. He created the affair as Abigail's prime motivator for accusing Elizabeth. Even though there was no historical record of it, Miller felt it appropriate based on information he read. Some critics have called the affair forced; others have seen it as a device that works.

Other reasons had also been known to prompt the people in Salem at the time to accuse fellow citizens of witchcraft. For example, victims of societal prejudice were accused first—a black slave from a faraway land and another woman who was poverty stricken and pregnant and unmarried. Similarly, prior to the trials, men were frequently creating reasons for suing landowners out of jealously because of their better livestock or land. Once the witch trials began, Thomas Putnam, it was said, told his daughter who to accuse in court, knowing that he would be able to purchase the convicted man's property while he was serving his sentence in prison. Another reason for an accusation was explained to Miller after *The Crucible* was produced. In a letter from a descendant of John Proctor, it was cited that Proctor was an amateur inventor of items that others found suspicious because of their ingenuity.

Some critics have accused Miller of inaccuracies in his portrayal of the Salem circumstances, and numerous essays have been written—both pro and con—on this topic. In the published play, Miller includes a note just prior to its beginning explaining that his goal was not to re-create an exact history, and he enumerates the changes he has made and why.

Over time, *The Crucible* has become Miller's most frequently produced play. Some critics see this as proof that the play is not just about the witch trials or McCarthyism but is universal. This, in fact, was Miller's goal, as he described it: "I wished for a way to write a play that would be sharp, that would lift out of the morass of subjectivism the squirming, single, defined process which would show that the sin of public terror is that it divests man of conscience, of himself."

Miller has written extensively on theater, and in a piece for the *New York Times* after *The Crucible* was completed but before it was produced, he voiced a similar viewpoint to the preceding one, although expressed in a different context. In the piece, he writes about the state of theater but makes no mention of *The Crucible*. He compares a negative force at work in the movie industry to one similar but less influential in theater, namely a practical, financial force to keep movies within certain boundaries and therefore similar and no longer risky. Miller describes it:

> But we [in the theater] have an atmosphere of dread just the same, an unconsciously—or consciously—accepted party line, a sanctified complex of moods and attitudes, proper and improper. If nothing else comes of it, one thing surely has: it has made it dangerous to dare, and, worse still, impractical. I am not speaking merely of political thought. Journalists have recently made studies of college students now in school and have been struck by the absence among them of any ferment, either religious, political, literary, or whatever. Wealthy, powerful, envied all about, it seems the American people stand mute.

List of Characters

Reverend Samuel Parris is a widower in his midforties who seems more concerned with his reputation as town minister than he is about his parishioners or his troubled daughter. He is repressive, insecure, vain, and paranoid. While he is quick to caution the townspeople against seeing his daughter as a witch, he is just as quick to support the authorities in condemning so many others once the witch trials commence.

Betty Parris is the minister's ten-year-old daughter, who has been caught dancing in the woods. Guilt-ridden and fearful of what may happen to her, she accuses others of being witches to cast blame elsewhere.

Tituba, a native of Barbados, is the slave in the Parris household and in her forties. She functions as an example of the downtrodden who are made into an easy target for blame; looked down upon for being black, she is thought to be the cause of Betty Parris's "illness" and is the first to be accused of witchcraft when the suspicious townspeople notice unexplainable things are happening.

Abigail Williams is Parris's beautiful seventeen-year-old orphaned niece who lives with his family. She was previously employed by the Proctors, and while there she tempted John Proctor. Powerful, manipulative, and evil, she sees goodness as a sham, needs to cover her mistakes, and is willing to commit murder to get what she wants. She leads the girls in their accusations in court against some of the most well-respected and good townspeople.

Mrs. Ann Putnam, wife of Thomas, is described as "a twisted soul of forty-five." Seven of her children have died as babies, and since she cannot understand a reason for their deaths and is superstitious, she believes a murdering witch is responsible.

Thomas Putnam is nearly fifty, the oldest son of the town's richest man, and highly vindictive. He is a prime example of evil in the village, believing himself superior to most and looking for revenge for past grievances. He has attempted to use force to get his way in the past but has always failed. Deeply embittered, he accuses many of being witches, frequently is a witness against those accused, and has a daughter who at times leads the hysterical girls in the finger pointing.

Mary Warren is the Proctor family's weak and impressionable seventeen-year-old servant. Initially awed by Abigail's strength, she later summons the courage to call the girls frauds in court but then again succumbs to their evil pressures.

John Proctor is an independent-minded, well-respected, strong Salem farmer in his midthirties and the main protagonist. He is plagued with guilt over a secret. Alternately labeled "very human" or "too good" by drama critics, no one denies he is transformed as the play progresses.

Rebecca Nurse is the ultimate good, religious community member. She takes on a near godlike aura when she first appears onstage and quiets a troubled child merely by her loving, calm presence.

Francis Nurse is the highly regarded resident of Salem who organizes a petition in support of his accused wife.

Giles Corey is in his early eighties, "a crank and a nuisance" who is constantly blamed for numerous things that go wrong in the town but is not guilty. Corey is independent and brave, someone who can reinforce the beliefs of Proctor yet who cannot serve as too strong of an aid because of his foibles.

Reverend John Hale, almost forty, is from a nearby town and is the recognized authority on witchcraft. He depends on information from books that he believes hold all the answers. Initially he is intent on doing good but does not realize the trouble he has helped create. He is one of the more developed characters to experience a change over the course of the play but becomes enlightened too late.

Elizabeth Proctor is first presented as the aggrieved wife of John and later as loving and understanding. Throughout the play, the community views her as one of its upright members, but she is more complex than a stereotype of goodness. She recognizes her faults and asks her husband for forgiveness, seeing herself as contributing to his own transgressions.

Ezekiel Cheever is a marshal of the court whose unquestioned obedience to authority leads him to gather "evidence" for the trial and comply with every order.

Judge Hathorne is one of the officials sent to question the accused witches. He is in his sixties, bitter, remorseless, and the foil for Proctor and the upright citizens. He is concerned more with his power than true justice, charging those who bring new evidence to court as being in contempt. In hindsight, Miller said he would have made this character even more evil.

Deputy Governor Danforth is the judge overseeing the witch trials in the highest court of the government of the province. In his sixties, grave and intent on upholding the power of the state at all costs, he is intelligent and at times open-minded but seduced by the girls' demonstration in court. In describing his court and how questioning proceeds, he says, "We burn a hot fire here."

Marshal Herrick is a man in his early thirties who works for the court yet feels some sympathy for those accused.

Summary and Analysis

While throughout the play there are several notes from Miller, usually providing background on characters, the longest of these occurs at the opening to **act 1**. Here, however, the focus is on the community and its history, rather than the characters in the play. We are taken to the spring of 1692 in Salem, Massachusetts, a time of great austerity and discipline, when undying work was required just to cultivate the land and make a living in this still-new world. The Puritan parents of these settlers had been persecuted in England, and, ironically, these descendants now rejected other religions as well, to keep their ways preserved from "wrong ways and deceitful ideas."

For these people, there was a great value in community, since there was still an element of danger in this land that was on the edge of unconquered wilderness. Yet at the same time the danger was starting to lessen and, as a result, some of the rules were disturbing to those more independent-minded inhabitants such as the main character of the play. A questioning of the usual systems and pressure for signs of greater individual freedom were what caused unease among many. This set the stage for the witch hunts, which, in an area where nearly all inhabitants knew the business of everyone else, also provided a most perverse outlet for expressing long-standing hatred of certain neighbors as well as jealousy against those with good or extensive land and livestock.

The **first scene** in act 1 opens in a bedroom in Reverend Samuel Parris's house, where Parris's daughter, Betty, is lying in bed completely still and he is kneeling next to her, praying and crying. He is interrupted by his slave, Tituba, whose only concern seems to be for Betty's welfare, yet Parris drives her out of the room. Next his niece Abigail enters and then Susanna Walcott, who brings a message from the doctor that he cannot find a remedy for Betty and believes her illness may have been brought on by "unnatural causes," that is, witchcraft. Parris looks at Susanna wide-eyed and tells her that this is not so and that he has sent for Reverend Hale to confirm it. He asks that she tell the doctor to keep consulting his books for a treatment.

When Susanna leaves, Abigail tells her uncle that many of the townspeople have heard about Betty's plight and the witchcraft rumor and a crowd has gathered in the parlor, waiting for an explanation. Now he presses Abigail, and we learn of the events that precipitated Betty's illness. Parris insists that Abigail tell him the truth before his enemies, who want to remove him as minister, learn it on their own. Parris tells her he saw the girls dancing in the "heathen" woods. Abigail swears they were only dancing and nothing else happened in the woods. He then tells her he saw Tituba waving her arms over the fire and screeching gibberish, to which Abigail explains that she was just singing her usual Barbados songs. Parris adds that he saw a dress on the ground and perhaps someone running naked, at which point the teenager is terrified and denies that anyone was naked.

Parris turns to another issue and asks his niece if there is any blemish on her own reputation, to which she responds that there is none. He has heard people say that Goody Proctor, who discharged Abigail from employment in the Proctor home, has hardly attended church, to avoid being near Abigail, whom she describes as "something soiled." Abigail explains that Goody hates her because Abigail would not be her slave and that Goody is a bitter, horrible woman. But Parris notes that no one else has tried to hire Abigail in the seven months since she was dismissed. At this point, Abigail's temper shows as she denies the charge again and again calls Goody a liar. The scene between Abigail and her uncle is reminiscent of a courtroom scene and certainly provokes some of the tension we imagine will arise later in the play. Also, the scene reveals Parris's suspicion of Abigail, even though he is her uncle; this coupled with her behavior makes the reader suspicious of her as well. Similarly, we become uneasy at the range of her responses, which change from somewhat deferential to quick-tempered.

The questioning is interrupted when Mrs. Ann Putnam enters and shortly thereafter her husband, Thomas Putnam. Both of the Putnams believe witchcraft is at work, although

Parris vehemently denies it. The Putnams also say that their daughter is in a bad state, walking but unable to see, hear, or eat.

In the written play, Miller interrupts the action to provide background on Thomas Putnam, "a man with many grievances." Putnam is the oldest son of the richest man in town and believes himself superior to most. Among other things, he is still quite angry that the town turned against the candidate he had proposed for minister of Salem, his brother-in-law. Relying on his usual forcefulness, Putnam had also failed to change his father's will, which left more money to Putnam's stepbrother than to him. In reaction, Putnam accuses many of witchcraft once the panic sets in the town, is a witness against the accused in many of the trials, and has a daughter who provokes other girls to testify against the accused as well.

We return to the action as Mrs. Putnam, at her husband's prompting, explains to Parris that she has had seven babies die and that Ruth, the only child still alive, had recently not been herself. To get to the bottom of the unusual circumstances, Mrs. Putnam sent Ruth to Tituba, so Tituba could connect her to speak with the dead children. Parris is astounded at the story and reminds Mrs. Putnam that such an action is a "formidable sin," which lets the audience know that the Puritans have other superstitions as well as believing in witches. Mrs. Putnam believes Ruth did connect with her dead siblings.

Parris turns to Abigail and accuses her of conjuring spirits, but she says it was only Tituba and Ruth who were involved. Abigail hopes to absolve herself, but, of course, we realize that she is not guiltless, since she never told Parris this version when he had previously questioned her. Earlier Parris had reminded Abigail that he has taken her in and cared for her, and again he reminds her of how poorly she has repaid him.

Putnam makes the suggestion that Parris, now even more fearful, should admit what happened to the people gathered, rather than wait for their accusations against those in his house. Parris still believes he is doomed, but his exclamations are interrupted when the Putnams' servant, Mercy Lewis, enters and tells them that Ruth Putnam is a little better. Putnam again urges Parris to speak to the villagers downstairs, and finally Parris agrees only to pray with them but not to mention witchcraft.

Abigail is left in the room with only Mercy Lewis. Abigail, scared, goes to Betty and shakes her and yells at her, "Now stop this! Betty! Sit up now!" But Betty remains limp. Abigail tells Mercy that if she is questioned she should say that the girls were dancing in the woods. Mercy replies, "Aye. And what more?" Abigail adds that Parris also knows that Tituba was conjuring Ruth's sisters. Mercy again asks, "And what more?" Abigail tells her that Parris saw Mercy naked. Again, we see the lack of straightforwardness in Abigail. She only provides a piece of information with each "And what more?" that comes from Mercy. Also, we see Abigail lie when she is not even pressured, for Parris only said he saw a dress, but never said he saw Mercy naked.

Mary Warren enters breathless and asks the two girls what they should do now that the entire village believes there are witches about. Before waiting for their answers, Mary says they must tell what occurred, since witches are hanged and Abigail would only get whipped for the dancing. Abigail exclaims, "Oh, *we'll* be whipped!" But Mary quickly reminds her that she only watched the others. Mercy moves toward her threateningly, and then a sound is heard from Betty. Abigail goes over to her and asks her to wake up. She sits Betty up and shakes her violently, yelling "I'll beat you, Betty!" Again she lies, telling Betty that she has told Parris everything, in an attempt to keep the girl from fearing her fate.

But Betty jumps up and runs toward the window, saying she will fly to her dead mother. Abigail prevents Betty from jumping and again says that she has told Parris everything. But Betty is not so sickly as she seems, for she screams out that Abigail drank blood, a charm to kill John Proctor's wife, and that Abigail never told Parris this. With this, Abigail "smashes her across the face." Betty collapses into the bed, sobbing and crying for her mother. Abigail repeats to the girls what they are allowed to reveal—only that they danced and it was Tituba who did the conjuring. She warns the girls that she can seriously harm them, having seen Indians smash the heads of her own parents. Mary Warren becomes hysterically frightened.

John Proctor enters the room. He is a farmer who has little patience for hypocrites, is rather independent, and is in his prime, confident, and strong. He yells for Mary to go home, and Mercy, too, is intimidated by him and leaves. Proctor goes to Betty, saying he has come to see what the town's uproar is about, and Abigail tells him just what she instructed the other girls to say about what happened. Abigail keeps moving closer to Proctor, telling him she's been waiting for him every night, to which he retorts that he has never given her justification for doing so. She reminds him of how he clutched her and says she knows he loved her then and still does, but he tells her she's speaking wildly, that he's hardly stepped off his farm for months. As she continues pushing him, he does admit that he has looked up at her bedroom window. With this, Abigail softens and starts to cry, then grabs him desperately again. When he gently pushes her away and starts to speak sympathetically, addressing her as "Child," she becomes quite angry.

John is pushed to anger, too, when Abigail starts to remark on the cruel coldness of his wife. Finally, he shakes her, and they hear the singing of a psalm from below, while Abigail, in tears, explains how she watches for the return of John Proctor, who enlightened her about the hypocrisy of the townspeople and their religion. So, theirs was not just a lustful relationship; Abigail believes he showed her the truth.

But as Proctor abruptly starts to leave, Betty suddenly covers her ears and moans loudly, causing her father to rush in, along with Mrs. Putnam, her husband, and Mercy. Rebecca Nurse enters, a woman of seventy-two who is highly respected in the community yet also has enemies because her husband had earned a great amount of land, which provoked great fights with neighbors, one of whom was a Putnam. By this time, another older person has entered as well—Giles Corey, a strong eighty-three-year-old. All are quiet as Rebecca, exuding gentleness, nears Betty's bed. The girl calms down and is quiet as others in the room are astonished. Rebecca explains that she has numerous children and grandchildren of her own. She advises, "A child's spirit is like a child, you can never catch it by running after it; you must stand still, and, for love, it will soon itself come back." Proctor is the only one in the room who is in agreement with Rebecca; clearly these two already stand out from the other foolish and overly emotional characters.

As the scene unfolds, Proctor questions why Parris made the decision to send for Reverend Hale without consulting the villagers, to which Parris replies that he is sick of meetings. Mrs. Putnam again brings up all of the children she's lost, and now she can compare her tragedy to the smooth life of Rebecca, who has eleven children and twenty-six grandchildren. The comparisons and accusations grow here, with Mr. Putnam standing up for Parris. Putnam accuses Proctor of not being a good Christian, since he has not seen him at their Sabbath meetings for months, but Proctor explains that this is because Parris speaks only of damnation in his preachings and hardly ever of God.

Those in the room persist in arguing, with Proctor, Rebecca, and Corey usually voicing agreement against the others. Parris complains that he has not gotten the wood to keep himself warm, but the others explain that his salary includes extra money so he can buy wood. Proctor admonishes him for being the first minister ever to ask them for the deed to the meeting house, and finally, Parris, fed up, furiously tells him they are not Quakers and he should tell his followers so. At this Proctor asks who these followers are, and Putnam explains that there is a group against Parris and "all authority!" To this Proctor retorts that he, then, must go find the group, and all are shocked.

Rebecca tries to take the heat off Proctor by saying that he really did not mean what he said, but he counters, "I mean it solemnly, Rebecca; I like not the smell of this "'authority.'" When Rebecca urges him to not "break charity" with Parris, he says he must go and get to work sowing and dragging home lumber, but even this simple comment can provide no easy escape, for Putnam accuses him of taking lumber from property that does not belong to him. Corey, who has just commented that there are too many fights and suings among the townspeople, says he too must go to work and tells Putnam they will win if Putnam dare fight them over the wood.

The bickering and reproach seem impossible to stop, and the Reverend Hale—the topic of the initial argument—enters the room. Again, Arthur Miller interrupts the written drama with a long description, this time providing some history of people's beliefs about the devil. For the Puritans, these beliefs also became entangled with politics, Miller explains. He also scoffs at the idea, which numerous critics have complained about, that the analogy between the fear of witches and fear of communists is not valid, since witches could not exist but communists do. But, Miller explains, he has no doubt that people in 1692 Salem "*were* communing with, and even worshiping," the devil.

Hale is carrying a stack of heavy books, which he describes as needing to be heavy since "they are weighted with authority." The use of "authority," of course, draws us back to Proctor's use of it just shortly before, when he voiced his concern over Parris's seeming belief that one authority stands for all authority, which should never be questioned. Hale enters, then, reinforcing the belief that authority has weight and therefore validity; he does not question what these books contain.

The first person Hale recognizes is Rebecca Nurse, whom he says he recognizes because of her reputation for goodness— she indeed looks like a good soul. This, of course, reinforces our view of her but does not say much for the other women in the room. Parris then introduces the Putnams, since he sees Putnam as an ally, and Hale exclaims over being in their "distinguished company." Hale immediately appears, then, not to favor one or the other of the camps that previously had shown themselves. John Proctor is cordial to Hale but slights the villagers and embarrasses Hale in the process, when he says that, since Hale is known to be a sensible man, it would be beneficial to the town if he would leave some of that sensibility in Salem. With this, Proctor leaves, perhaps proving Corey's earlier statement that Proctor does not believe in witches, although Proctor had denied ever making such a statement.

The others left in the room immediately start to tell Hale of the unusual things they have seen, seemingly indicating witchcraft, but Hale quickly warns them that he is here to make such judgments and will not proceed unless they promise to believe his findings once he has garnered all the facts. While

Hale, so far, has been described as wanting to do what is good and right, we see that he also fits into another category where Parris, too, resides, which is the category of authority that can never be questioned. This immediately serves as a warning to the audience that we are again in dangerous territory, since Hale is not necessarily the purely sensible man of reputation.

In the course of enumerating for Hale the various unusual events that the townspeople have no explanations for, Mrs. Putnam adds that she ordered her daughter to go to Tituba to conjure up the dead in an attempt to get some answers, which shocks Rebecca Nurse. Again we see dissension among the townspeople as Mrs. Putnam warns Nurse that, "I'll not have you judging me any more!" Hale listens intently and goes to his books for answers as all wait attentively, yet he provides no explanation of what he will do, but only repeats that his books have all the answers and that he will crush the devil if he is indeed among them. Rebecca is the only one to ask if the child might be hurt in the process. When Hale tells her it might be a brutal procedure, she says she must go and that she will go to God for Parris. He immediately questions her, fearfully and with resentment, "I hope you do not mean we go to Satan here!" The others, too, are resentful of her seeming superiority, again showing the disagreeableness in the town and pointing to the dividing line between the groups. Giles Corey is the only one left in the room from the Proctor/Nurse/Corey contingent. At this point, Miller interrupts the action in the written play to insert a description of Corey—a nuisance who is blamed for nearly every problem in the town yet who is innocent, independent, and very brave.

Hale turns to Betty, asking who has afflicted her, but when the girl remains limp, he turns, with narrowing eyes, to Abigail. As in the opening of the play, when Parris questioned Abigail alone, here again, new tidbits of information emerge. We learn that in the woods the girls danced around a kettle that a frog supposedly jumped into. The pressure increases on Abigail, with Hale reminding her that her cousin may be dying, and Abigail calls out Tituba's name, as if she is the only guilty party. Mrs. Putnam leaves to get Tituba, while Hale continues to pressure Abigail, to the point that when Tituba enters Abigail immediately proclaims that Tituba makes her drink blood.

When Tituba admits she has given Abigail chicken blood, Hale pounces on her with questions. Abigail interjects with more accusations against Tituba, saying the slave has made her laugh at prayers, corrupted her dreams, and tempted her. All in the room are against Tituba now, and when Tituba explains that Abigail asks her to conjure spirits and make charms, we realize that Tituba is telling the truth, since we know, although the others on stage do not, that earlier Betty revealed this as well.

The intensity rises as Parris says Tituba must confess or he will whip her to death. While we assume this is a metaphor rather than a literal promise, the punishment immediately intensifies, as Putnam cries that she must be hanged. Tituba is now terrified and weeping and suggests that someone else may be bewitching the children. With this new comment to latch on to, Hale and Parris squeeze Tituba for names of these others who are cavorting with the devil. The evil Putnam suggests the names of two women from the village. Hale explains that Tituba will be protected by God, who has made her an instrument for discovering the devil's agents. It seems that if she provides this information she may be safe.

First, Tituba, "in a fury," says the devil has repeatedly requested that she kill Parris, since he is a mean man, but she has turned down his demand, even though he has offered much temptation, because she does not hate Parris. Undoubtedly she believes this story may save her, yet when all it does is inspire gasps from those gathered, she proceeds to give them what they've requested—names of supposedly guilty community members. She says Sarah Good and Goody Osburn—the very two people Putnam had suggested before—belong to the devil. Mrs. Putnam reveals that Goody Osburn had delivered three of her children who died; now we understand why Putnam had chosen her name earlier.

Hale again tells Tituba that she will be blessed for any help she can provide, and with this Abigail cries out, staring and enraptured, "I want to open myself!" She now admits that she danced with the devil but wants to return to Jesus.

She reiterates the two names Tituba has announced as being fellow conspirators with the devil and adds another. With this, Betty gets up from bed, staring, and rattles off two more guilty villagers' names. Parris and Hale are thrilled that Betty is back, but Betty still calls out another name, and so does Abigail, back and forth until a total of eleven people are accused. The only thing that seems to end their "ecstatic cries" of more names is the curtain falling to show the end of act 1. It should be noted that many have postulated that in the nonfictional Salem of 1692 the repressive society drove the girls to dance in the woods, that personal vendettas caused some of the accusations, as did the realization that once someone was jailed and condemned his property would be made available for sale to the other villagers.

Act 2 opens eight days later in the empty living room at the Proctor home, a sharply different setting than the previous crowded and chaotic Parris bedroom. Elizabeth is heard singing softly to her children upstairs, and Proctor enters from outside carrying a gun. The contrast between them is immediately set. Elizabeth suspiciously asks him why he is so late coming home and fears he has been in Salem visiting Abigail. Proctor tells Elizabeth he wants to please her, rises and kisses her, but receives a lukewarm response and is disappointed. More of his sensitive side is displayed as he says they need flowers in the house, and when he looks out the door and poetically comments on the beauty of the lilacs.

Details of events outside the home begin to surface. Elizabeth says that Mary Warren is in Salem, which angers Proctor, since he forbade Mary to attend the trial and since he sees it as a sign of his wife's weakness that she allowed Mary to go. But Elizabeth explains that Mary proudly announced that she must go, since she is now an official of the court. This is the first Proctor's heard of a special court being in place, and his wife explains that there are four judges in from Boston as well as the deputy governor of the province, who is in charge. Fourteen people are already in jail and could be hanged. Proctor scoffs at the unlikeliness of this occurring, but his wife quotes the deputy governor's promise to hang those who do not confess. Abigail and the other girls are greatly respected now, and people are declared guilty based on if the girls "scream and howl and fall to the floor" as if bewitched by the person before them.

Proctor is "wide-eyed," and Elizabeth tells him he must go to Salem and inform the court of his conversation with Abigail and her admission at her uncle's house that the strange incidents had nothing to do with witchcraft. Proctor hesitates, stating, "I am only wondering how I may prove what she told me, Elizabeth," he explains. "If the girl's a saint now, I think it is not easy to prove she's fraud, and the town gone so silly. She told it to me in a room alone—I have no proof for it." Elizabeth becomes increasingly suspicious of Proctor's having an affair as he rationalizes his hesitancy to reveal Abigail. Proctor's comment also brings to the forefront the tension between the husband and wife. He is angry about her suspicions and warns her not to judge him, saying he has been so careful to please his wife ever since Abigail left seven months ago. When he enters his house, he says, it is like entering a court (a formidable comparison, since we know the newly set up court in Salem is out of control). Yet even though he is angry, Elizabeth, whom he had earlier accused of being too weak in dealing with Mary Warren, will not relent when she realizes he has not been honest with her.

This stressful atmosphere is interrupted by Mary Warren, who serves only to heighten the negativity and tension. Immediately upon her entrance, Proctor confronts her for going to Salem, which he has expressly forbidden. He rebukes her for not getting her work done, especially since his wife has not been completely well. Oddly, Mary gives a doll she has made in court to Elizabeth as a present and remarks, "We must all love each other now." She wants to go to bed, but when Proctor asks her if it is true that fourteen women are now jailed, she lets them know that now there are thirty-nine. She starts sobbing and tells them that Goody Osburn is to be hanged but that Sarah Good will get off easier since she confessed to making a deal with the devil.

Mary says that in court Sarah Good tried to choke all the girls to death with her spirit and that, in fact, the woman tried to kill her many times before this. The Proctors keep questioning her, and Mary explains that she felt sorry for the old woman who is so poor that she sleeps in ditches. But then Mary provides a flimsy explanation of why she turned against the woman and why the judges condemned her as well. We find out also that Sarah Good smokes a pipe and that even though she is almost sixty, she is pregnant and husbandless, additional reasons for the upright Puritans to be against her.

Mary repeats that she is an official in court and will have to be gone daily, at which Proctor takes down his whip and Elizabeth tries to talk sense into the girl. Mary cowers from Proctor, and just as he raises the whip and reaches for her she points to Elizabeth, yelling, "I saved her life today!" With this, the whip drops and the couple finds out that Elizabeth's name had been mentioned in court but that Mary stood up for her and the judges dropped the inquiry. Mary says that by law she is not to reveal who brought up Elizabeth's name. This girl, who had earlier been described as quite mousy, now realizes she has power and turns to Proctor to make it clear to him, telling him that he now must treat her better and letting him know that she and the other girls just had dinner with the judges and deputy governor.

Once Mary goes to bed, Proctor and Elizabeth are left staring. "Oh, the noose, the noose is up!" Elizabeth says to her husband. She is trembling as they try to decide what to do, both believing she is only temporarily safe. Elizabeth asks her husband to go to Abigail and break her illusion, since it is clear that the girl believes that Proctor would marry her if Elizabeth were gone. There is great tension, and Proctor is angry and again disturbed that his wife sees him as deceitful, as if he promised Abigail something when they were together. "When will you know me, woman? Were I stone I would have cracked for shame this seven month!" he tells her.

As Proctor prepares to leave, Reverend Hale appears in the doorway, now more deferential, drawn, and perhaps feeling slightly guilty. The couple is shocked and frightened to see him as he is there out of his own concern and not on official business. "I am a stranger here, as you know," he reminds them.

"And in my ignorance I find it hard to draw a clear opinion of them that come accused before the court." This is a reversal in character from act 1, when he was completely confident that his books held all the answers. Hale tells them that he has just come from Rebecca Nurse's house because her name has been mentioned in court, even though he knows she will never be accused. This disturbs the couple further, since they know Rebecca is one of the most devout people in the village.

Hale explains that he would like to determine "the Christian character" of the Proctor house, and Proctor is immediately resentful but knows he must go along with the visitor. Hale asks why Proctor has been so infrequently at church and why his third child has not been baptized; Proctor explains that his poor opinion of Parris has dictated these actions, and this seems reasonable in light of what we saw of Parris in act 1. Hale still feels uncertain about these explanations, however, and asks if the couple know their commandments. Proctor proceeds to list them, but he cannot recall the commandment against committing adultery; his wife must remind him, causing more distress and pain for him to hear it pass through his wife's lips.

It is clear that Hale has misgivings about the Proctors, and Elizabeth, wanting to change his impression, asks her husband to tell Hale his information. Proctor, with trouble, tells Hale that Abigail said the excursion in the woods had nothing to do with witchcraft. Hale is shocked, and Proctor reminds him that many may confess to avoid hanging, not because it is the truth. Proctor explains as well his concern about going to court with this information, since the court has been so willing to convict good, upright people. Hale finally is impressed with Proctor, yet he brings up one more point, which is whether Proctor believes in witches at all. This time, though, Hale is disturbed by Elizabeth's answers, and her husband stands up for her.

Hale prepares to leave, but now Giles Corey is in the doorway and tells them his wife has been taken to jail. Directly behind him is Francis Nurse, whose wife has also been arrested. "They've surely gone wild now, Mr. Hale!" Elizabeth proclaims, and the others turn to Hale as well, desperate for help. Hale, while deeply troubled, has some understanding of these people but still has faith in the judges: "Believe me, Mr. Nurse, if Rebecca Nurse be tainted, then nothing's left to stop the whole green world from burning. Let you rest upon the justice of the court; the court will send her home, I know it." Ezekiel Cheever then appears in the door with a warrant for Elizabeth's arrest, and Proctor immediately turns to Hale, who had just told them there were no charges against her.

Cheever says that he has been given warrants only just that night for sixteen more people, that Abigail has charged Elizabeth, and that he is to search their home for any poppets (rag dolls). Cheever says he does not want to search, and the Proctors say they have no such things, but he spies one on their mantel, the one that Mary had brought home that evening. Proctor says his wife will not go, and he sends her off to get Mary. Cheever examines the doll and is distressed when he finds a needle in it, explaining that at dinner that evening Abigail had screamed in pain and Parris had found a needle stuck two inches inside her belly. Abigail said Elizabeth's spirit had put it there. The clerk calls it "hard proof," and Hale seems in agreement.

When Mary appears, Proctor and Hale question her, and she admits she brought the poppet home and had put the needle in herself. Elizabeth is shocked to hear the story about Abigail, speaks out in horror against her, and Cheever takes note. Proctor grabs the warrant from his hand, rips it, and yells for Cheever and Hale to leave his house, calling Hale "a broken minister" for never once questioning the innocence of Abigail or Parris and for not recognizing that these accusations are prompted by vengeance.

After this outburst, Elizabeth says she will go, and Proctor is warned that there are nine men outside to help with the arrests. Proctor again appeals to Hale that she should not be taken, and when Hale starts to reply that the courts are just, Proctor yells, "Pontius Pilate! God will not let you wash your hands of this!" Elizabeth is severely shaken, and Proctor promises to get her out of jail as soon as she leaves the house. When he hears clanking chains, he chases after the men, cursing them and yelling that they cannot chain her. Now Corey berates Hale, "And yet silent, minister? It is fraud, you know it is fraud!

What keeps you, man?" Proctor is forced back inside by three men and screams after them that he will get revenge.

Hale advises the husbands that they must think of evidence that can be brought to court to counter the charges against their wives. Corey and Nurse depart, and Proctor tells Mary they must go to court together, so she can explain what happened with the doll and needle. Mary is more frightened and says she cannot do it. "She'll kill me for sayin' that!" she says and adds, "Abby'll charge lechery on you, Mr. Proctor!" He is shocked that Mary knows about this but stops advancing toward her only for a moment. Now, in addition to being angry he is confronted with his own hatred of himself. "Good. Then her saintliness is done with," he says. "We will slide together into our pit. . . ." Proctor catches Mary as she repeats that she cannot go; he grabs her throat as if to strangle her and then throws her down. She sobs and continues calling out, "I cannot, I cannot. . . ." as the curtain falls.

Arthur Miller added act 2, scene 2 to the play near the end of its run on Broadway. Many have said it is unnecessary both dramatically and thematically, and the play has been performed with and without it and sometimes as **act 3, scene 1**. Laurence Olivier, while supposedly initially a fan of this insertion, later told Miller that while it expands the reader's perspective, in the performed play it destroys the underlying "marching tempo" and insistent "drumbeat." Some have said that the scene provides more information about Abigail and reveals more about her relationship with Proctor.

Proctor and Abigail meet in the woods, and Proctor is surprised that she is dismayed to be receiving so much negative attention. She tells him she is suffering from the pinholes on her leg and arm and touches her stomach to show she is still not healed from Elizabeth's jabs there. Proctor sees her now as mad. She tells him that the town is full of evil hypocrites and that she will speak out against many more villagers. When Proctor asks her if there is anyone good, she says he is—that he taught her goodness and removed her ignorance. God has given her the strength to get rid of them, she tells him, and she promises to make him a good wife when the world is clean.

Proctor backs away from her and reminds her that his wife's trial is tomorrow and that she has been in jail for 36 days. He says he has come to tell Abigail what he plans to do in court at the trial, so that she might think of some way to save herself. But Proctor appears to have made a serious mistake. Instead of destroying Abigail's hope of ever being his wife, he goes to her and loses the advantage that he could have had in court, possibly putting his wife at greater risk. He tells Abigail he is giving her the opportunity to remove the charges against his wife, and to therefore prevent him from having to bring forth the damning evidence against Abigail and himself. Here Proctor is concerned with his wife gaining freedom, not with aiding any of his friends' wives or any of the others falsely accused. Indeed, this shows him as less heroic than he appears without the scene, and it addresses some critics' contentions that he is too good.

Abigail acts shocked. She cannot believe that to explain her vendetta against Elizabeth he will admit in court he had a sexual relationship with Abigail. Abigail laughs madly, trembling and looking at him as if he is mad. She says that he is hopeful his wife will die and that she will save him from himself in court the next day. Proctor is described as "amazed, in terror."

We go to the vestry room of the Salem meetinghouse, which is now used as the anteroom of the court. Depending upon the production, this is either the start of **act 3** or **act 3, scene 2**. The room is empty, quite somber, and "even forbidding." Through the wall we hear Martha Corey being accused of reading fortunes by Judge Hathorne. The stage setting indicates that she, like the others accused, are convicted based on unseen evidence. They are interrupted when Giles Corey yells out that he has evidence, and we also hear the excited voices of the gathered townspeople. Danforth calls for order, and when Corey will not be quiet, he is ordered removed by Herrick and appears in the anteroom before us. Hale leaves the court to come to Corey, and Corey tells him he must make the judge listen to him. Instead, Judge Hathorne enters, yelling at Corey and calling him "daft," but he is followed by Deputy Governor Danforth and all become quiet.

Danforth tells Corey that he must submit his evidence in proper affidavit form and orders the attendants to take him away. Yet before any dismissal, Francis Nurse speaks up, and when Danforth tells him as well to write his plea, Nurse proclaims that the girls the judges have been relying on are frauds. This disturbs Danforth, who asks if the man realizes that he has sent four hundred people to jail so far and that seventy-two are to be hanged.

The talk is interrupted when John Proctor enters, guiding Mary Warren by the elbow, as if "she were near collapse." Parris becomes fearful at seeing her, especially when Proctor says she has information for the deputy governor. Parris speaks out against Proctor, but Hale tells Danforth he "thinks" they "must" listen to her. Danforth is very interested and hears that Mary Warren is there to say that she never saw any spirits. Concerned, Danforth asks Proctor if he has revealed this information to anyone in the town and if he realizes that in these trials the court has contended that God is speaking through the children. He questions Mary, and she says that the other girls are pretending too, that none of the townspeople have set evil spirits against them.

Ezekiel Cheever and Parris attempt to discredit Proctor. Then Danforth offers him a deal. He tells Proctor that Elizabeth claims to be pregnant, and if she is he will spare her life for at least a year. Considering this, Danforth asks him if he still wants to go through with presenting his evidence and being questioned, to which Proctor says he will, since his friends' wives are still accused. This shows some of Proctor's heroism, since part of his testimony will require revealing his own sexual sin.

Proctor will be heard in the court, and, surprisingly, even though Parris and Hathorne have been railing against Corey, Nurse, and Proctor, now Marshal Herrick unexpectedly stands up for Proctor. First Proctor presents a list of townspeople who've signed a paper declaring Rebecca, Martha, and Elizabeth to be good and to have never shown signs that they were in concert with the devil. Ninety-one people have signed, and Parris, now sweating, says they should be called to court for questioning and declares that these people are intent on attacking the court. Hathorne also pushes for the people to be brought in, while Nurse and Hale are against it. Danforth orders Cheever to bring the people in, making Nurse horrified and guilt-stricken, since he says he promised all of these people that they would not get into any trouble. Mary Warren suddenly starts to sob.

Next Proctor shows Danforth Corey's deposition, which looks as though it has been prepared by a lawyer, but Corey explains that he did it himself, since he has often been unfairly accused and has had practice in court. He also tells Danforth that Danforth's father ruled in his favor many years earlier, which should be to Corey's benefit. Corey's deposition states that Thomas Putnam is manipulating the proceeding in order to gain land. Hathorne asks who gave Corey this information and the old man is shocked and says he cannot tell him, since this person will be thrown in jail as well. Hathorne declares that this is contempt of court. Proctor stands up for Corey, while Hathorne and Parris keep pushing for punishment. Finally Hale speaks up, reminding Danforth that the villagers now have an awful fear of the court. But Danforth retorts, "No uncorrupted man may fear this court, Mr. Hale! None!" This shows how out of touch Danforth is, as well as how consumed he is with having all obey him; it also shows a change taking hold of Hale, who not much earlier had also declared that the court should be trusted but now understands why the villagers fear doing so.

Danforth says Corey is under arrest for contempt of court. Corey lunges at Putnam, but Proctor holds him back, assuring him that their additional proof will sway the court. But Corey responds, "Say nothin' more, John. He's only playin' you! He means to hang us all!" This indicates the enormous power of the court not only to go forward with possibly killing the accused women but to destroy the men themselves as well and possibly others. Mary Warren bursts into sobs again, adding to the tension.

Proctor calms Mary and approaches Danforth to give him Mary's deposition, but Hale interrupts, saying that this testimony is so important that Proctor should have a lawyer. Hale pleads with Danforth, "Excellency, I have signed seventy-two death warrants; I am a minister of the Lord, and I dare not take a life without there be proof so immaculate no slightest qualm of conscience may doubt it." While Danforth listens to the pleas of Hale, he asks Hale twice if he questions Danforth's abilities to judge. Hale relents, and the proceedings that have seemed inevitable since early in act 2 begin.

Danforth and the others read Mary's deposition, and Danforth seems quite stirred. For the first time, he berates Parris for interrupting once again, another sign that Danforth may be moving towards favoring Proctor's story. Danforth questions Mary as to whether she is lying or Proctor pressured her to do so, but Mary denies both points. The other girls are brought into court, and Danforth tells them Mary claims that she never saw spirits or any sign of the devil and that neither did the other girls. He asks Abigail if this is true, and when she denies it, Danforth warns them: "Children, a very augur bit will now be turned into your souls until your honesty is proved."

The questioning starts on the issue of poppets. Abigail says, "with a slight note of indignation," that Mary is lying when she states that Abigail saw her make the poppet (that was later found at the Proctor house) in court and put the needle in the doll. Abigail says that Elizabeth always had poppets, which Proctor denies, and both Hathorne and Parris chime in against him, finally pushing a furious Proctor to take another approach. He questions what Mary has to gain by making these statements.

Danforth asks Proctor if he realizes that he is accusing Abigail of a murder plot, which Proctor states he understands, to Danforth's incredulity. Proctor then reveals other points that he knows the judges will find disturbing—that Abigail was removed from their religious services twice because she was laughing and that she and the other girls danced in the woods naked. Ironically, the judges say that laughing during services is irrelevant, even though the religious character of numerous others has been examined in detail; the irony stands out particularly in light of Hale's questioning of the Proctors at their home. As for the dancing in the woods, this creates an uproar, even pushing Hale to finally speak up, and Danforth sees that the situation "is growing into a nightmare."

The disturbed Danforth allows Hathorne to question Mary, and he turns the examination to Mary's fainting and turning cold in court, which she now says was all pretense. Hathorne states that if this were indeed pretense then Mary should show them now how she did it. Parris chimes in as well, calling for a demonstration, but Mary looks at Proctor and says she cannot, and he becomes quietly alarmed yet still encourages her to try. Part of the feeling that Salem has gone mad is even supported by the way the court is run; seemingly it is a free-for-all, with Danforth setting rules nearly at whim. Similarly, Danforth is not the only one doing the questioning; he has turned this over to Hathorne at this point, and even Parris is allowed to ask the girl questions. Additionally, the idea that those who confess to being witches will be let out of jail makes no sense, since these people who were believed to cause great harm will now be free to do so.

The tension is sustained through this act by the jockeying for Danforth's favor, which seems to sway back and forth as the testimony wears on. After being pressured, Mary explains that in court she got wrapped up in the commotion when the other girls started screaming and when she saw how Danforth himself believed the girls. Danforth now seems to understand Mary and, worried, he looks to Abigail and asks her if this is what motivated her, too, rather than the presence of actual spirits. Abigail answers, "Why, this—this—is a base question, sir," and throughout the rest of the act is seemingly insulted and disbelieving that she should have to undergo such questioning. She says that she cannot believe that she is mistrusted, and Danforth weakens. Also noteworthy is that she calls Danforth the more common "Mr.," rather than "Your Honor" or "Your Excellency" for example, as she boldly threatens: "Let *you* beware, Mr. Danforth. Think you to be so mighty that the power of Hell may not turn *your* wits? Beware of it!"

Abigail, looking frightened and shivering, turns her gaze upward and then looks at Mary as if she is responsible. The other girls follow Abigail's lead; their teeth chatter and they blame Mary for it. Mary emits a hysterical cry and starts to run but is caught by Proctor, who then leaps to Abigail, grabs her hair, and pulls her up to stand. She screams, along with Danforth and others in the room, as Proctor roars, "How do you call Heaven! Whore! Whore!" Proctor is pried away from her in agony, while Danforth is shocked. Trembling, Proctor confesses in two short sentences that he committed adultery with Abigail, and Danforth is now dumbfounded.

Greatly ashamed and with a breaking voice, Proctor explains that it happened about eight months ago, when Abigail worked at the Proctor home. Miller describes Proctor as clamping his jaw to keep from weeping as he continues. His wife dismissed Abigail, Proctor says, nearly overcome and trying to gain control. He turns away for a moment and then cries out about Abigail, "She thinks to dance with me on my wife's grave! And well she might, for I thought of her softly. God help me, I lusted, and there *is* a promise in such sweat. But it is a whore's vengeance, and you must see it; I set myself entirely in your hands. I know you must see it now."

Proctor is noble enough to willingly accept blame for his own actions. He uses nearly the same language his wife used with him earlier in act 2. She had advised him to understand that a woman might see the act as meaning something more than a man might, that the woman might believe the man will change his life for her, even if this is not directly stated. By using part of his wife's explanation, Proctor seems closer to her and understanding of her position. While he repeatedly uses the word "whore" to describe Abigail, though, he never uses similar language to describe himself, one of a number of reasons some feminists are critical of the play.

Danforth is horrified, and when he turns to Abigail to ask if she denies all that has just been told, she remains contemptuous, saying she must not answer, and threatens to leave. "I'll not have such looks!" she proclaims to Danforth and must be stopped from walking out. Following another tactic, Danforth asks that Elizabeth Proctor be brought into the court. Again Danforth asks John Proctor to completely clarify that his wife fired Abigail because she knew her to be a "harlot." To Abigail, Danforth issues a warning. He has both Abigail and Proctor turn their backs, so they will not face Elizabeth when she is in the room.

Following this preparation, Elizabeth is brought in and looks around the room for her husband. Danforth warns her to look only at him and asks why she dismissed Abigail from working in the Proctor home. Elizabeth is hesitant, not knowing how to answer the question, since she wants to tell the truth but does not want to cause her husband trouble. She does admit, "I thought I saw my husband somewhat turning from me," but she will not go so far as to say anything else against him. She is in agony, since Danforth will not drop the questioning and finally holds her face so she must look only at him. He asks directly if her husband is a lecher, to which she finally, quietly responds that he is not. Her husband calls out to her to tell the truth, telling her that he has already admitted it to the court. Now Elizabeth knows she has unwittingly caused problems, but she is escorted out before she can explain.

Danforth accuses Proctor of lying and Hale once more tries to speak on his behalf, pleading for him to bring Elizabeth back into the court. The chances of Danforth changing his mind diminish, however, when Abigail screams that she sees a yellow bird in the rafters—allegedly the spirit of Mary Warren trying to attack her. Mary protests this accusation, but the girls in the courtroom begin to mimic her, as if under her spell. The atmosphere in the courtroom intensifies as mass hysteria takes control. Proctor tries to comfort Mary, but she turns on him, calling him "the Devil's man!" Frantic, she claims that Proctor has hounded her and threatened her, quoting his supposed words: "'I'll murder you,' he says, 'if my wife hangs! We must go and overthrow the court,' he says!" She knows exactly the words to cause more horror, for all along Proctor and the others have been said to want to overthrow the court and make a mockery of its power, indicating how fragile the court and/or its supporters must be if there is constant fear of it being undermined.

Danforth turns against Proctor, who is dumbstruck with anger. Hale again attempts to implore Danforth, who immediately silences him. Danforth asks Proctor if he will confess. Proctor, wild and in disbelief over what has happened, says that God is dead. Parris calls out, reveling in the victory over this man, whose statement shows him, in Parris's eyes, to in fact not be an upright Christian. Proctor "laughs insanely" and then charges: "A fire, a fire is burning! I hear the boot of Lucifer, I see his filthy face! And it is my face, and yours, Danforth! For them that quail to bring men out of ignorance, as I have quailed, and as you quail now when you know in all your black hearts that this be fraud—God damns our kind especially, and we will burn, we will burn together!"

This pronouncement is striking for a number of reasons. First, even though Proctor realizes he and others are doomed, he speaks not of this but of his own guilt, showing how it has nearly destroyed him. He speaks of this even before he lashes out at Danforth, even though Danforth is grossly more guilty. Unusual as well is the fact that Proctor does not just condemn himself and then Danforth but that he puts them both in the same category. The hero has high standards for himself, and when he does not meet them he feels as low as the lowest. While some have criticized that Proctor is too good of a man, it seems we could also view his response here as a weakness, in that he sees his mistake as comparable to that of a man who is responsible for numerous condemnations and deaths.

Danforth calls for Proctor and Corey to be taken to jail. Proctor proclaims: "You are pulling Heaven down and raising up a whore!" Hale denounces the court and leaves, quitting his position. Danforth, who has hardly been open-minded with Hale, is now furious at losing him.

Act 4 opens that fall in a Salem jail cell. Herrick enters the cell shared by Tituba and Sarah Good. All around, the actions of the three show the strain and change that has taken place, even on these lesser characters. Tituba and Sarah Good speak in a mocking, almost delusional manner, as if they are indeed witches, and Herrick drinks liquor from a flask, giving Sarah some when she requests it. All are apparently worn from the last few months, as indicated by Herrick's remark to them that "it's the proper morning to fly into Hell."

Danforth, Hathorne and Cheever enter, and Danforth questions Herrick about the reappearance of Hale. Herrick explains that Hale has been speaking with those who are next to be hanged. Danforth is disturbed that Herrick has been drinking, and Danforth also comments, "There is a prodigious stench in this place," pushing us to assume that literally the jail is most unpleasant but that figuratively the whole place is in ruins. It is curious that Danforth himself makes the comment that can be read as a charge against his own self, although, of course, this is not his intention.

Before Herrick brings in Parris, there are hints of even further disarray as well as some revelations that are clear indications of additional problems. Something is going on in another town, Andover, but Danforth tells Hathorne not to speak of it. Also, Hathorne tells Danforth that Parris has had a mad look lately and that he has seen him weeping. Cheever explains that Parris is disturbed because of all the trouble in the village. He and other villagers are arguing now that many cows are wandering freely, since their masters are jailed and it is unclear who they will now belong to.

Parris enters, "gaunt, frightened, and sweating," and it is only now that we learn that Parris had called for Danforth. Danforth immediately berates Parris for allowing Hale into the jail, and Parris explains that it is actually a very beneficial occurrence, since Hale is trying to convince Rebecca Nurse and others to confess. Parris hesitates to tell Danforth something more that apparently is on his mind, but Danforth says he must. Parris says that Abigail has taken off, he is pretty sure, to board a ship with Mercy Lewis, and has robbed him of all his money. He explains that he believes they were motivated to protect themselves, having heard of what happened in Andover. Yet Danforth still wants to hear nothing of Andover, even though Parris explains that rumors are circulating in Salem that there has been a revolt in that town. Danforth is angry, and denies this, yet Parris still tells him what the people in Salem have heard—that people in Andover overthrew the court and ended all talk of witchcraft. Parris warns that the same might happen in Salem.

Parris explains that since they are ready to hang the most upright citizens of Salem, the villagers have a notably different perspective of the court. Hathorne is greatly concerned and asks Parris if he has advice, to which Parris replies that they should postpone the hangings. Danforth immediately says this is not possible, but Parris explains further that now that Hale is speaking to the prisoners there may be a chance that at least one will confess, which should thereby force the villagers to accept that the court is right in its judgment of all imprisoned. Parris adds that only thirty people attended Proctor's excommunication.

But Danforth will not give in and tells Parris that he himself will go and try to persuade one of the prisoners to confess. Parris warns that he will not have enough time, since the group is scheduled to be executed at dawn. Still Danforth will not be swayed. Then Parris describes another frightening occurrence, saying that when he opened his door to leave his home a dagger fell. Now we understand why Parris has been so concerned about the hangings; he tells Danforth that he is in great danger, and we see him as unchanged in his self-centeredness.

Hale enters, exhausted and pained by sorrow. He immediately tells Danforth that he must pardon the prisoners. When Danforth remains unmoved, Hale asks for more time with the prisoners to convince them to confess. Yet Danforth is insistently against this, sticking to a weak explanation: "Twelve are already executed; the names of these seven are given out, and the village expects to see them die this morning. Postponement now speaks a floundering on my part; reprieve or pardon must cast doubt upon the guilt of them that died till now." Danforth rationalizes here in the name of being fair to all, not accepting that, if there has been a mistake in the accusations, the moral man would stop the deaths now before many more are unfairly executed.

Danforth is prepared for a fight if the villagers provoke it, and he tries to calm Parris and Hale by stating, "If retaliation is your fear, know this—I should hang ten thousand that dared to rise against the law, and an ocean of salt tears could not melt the resolution of the statutes." Danforth decides he will take on convincing John Proctor to confess. In making the decision about who to attempt to persuade, it is curious that Danforth does not consider the testimony against the various prisoners but only if there is some hope of convincing the person and if Hale had already made an attempt with the individual.

Danforth thinks it best to first have Elizabeth urge her husband to confess. While the group waits for Elizabeth to be brought before them, Hale tries again to change Danforth's mind. He tells him he will not be seen as weak but as merciful if he postpones the executions. But Hale does not understand that Danforth has no desire to be viewed as merciful. Hale also reminds Danforth that he may be responsible for causing a rebellion, and when Hale realizes he now has Danforth's attention he describes the chaotic state of the village, where orphans are wandering about, cattle are loose, and crops lie stinking and rotting in the fields. He warns Danforth, "[Y]ou wonder yet if rebellion's spoke? Better you should marvel how they do not burn your province!" Danforth asks him if he has preached in Andover recently, assuming that has riled Hale, but Hale says he hasn't. When Danforth says he cannot understand why, then, Hale has returned, Hale first answers sarcastically and then speaks of his own guilt. "There is blood on my head! Can you not see the blood on my head!!" It seems fitting that there are exclamation points after this second sentence rather than question marks, for there is no point in asking Danforth such a question; he refuses to see his own horrific mistakes and so could hardly see Hale's.

Elizabeth enters, looking poorly, and while Danforth starts to speak with her, he realizes his forte is cross-examination, and asks Hale to proceed instead. Hale explains to Elizabeth that he no longer is associated with the court and wishes Proctor's life could be spared; if it is not, he feels he is his murderer. Hale says that as a Christian he has struggled with the idea of trying to convince those who are jailed to confess and thereby lie. Hathorne denies that lying is involved, but Hale retorts that it would be lying since the people are innocent. Danforth says there can be no more such talk.

Hale begs Elizabeth to induce her husband to confess, telling her that there is no justification for taking a life and that God may damn a liar who confesses less than he would a person "that throws his life away for pride." But Elizabeth quietly states that this sounds like the devil's argument, a curious choice of words, since the men surrounding her are supposedly responsible for determining who is in allegiance with the devil and since John Proctor himself already accused Danforth of being the devil's advocate for accusing so many.

Since Hale is not making progress with Elizabeth, Danforth steps in, attempting to appeal purely to her emotional side. Yet he is surprised to see Elizabeth being unresponsive and unemotional. Just when he loses his patience with her, she says she will speak with her husband but will not promise that she will urge him to confess. John Proctor is brought to the cell, no longer appearing like himself but instead dirty and bearded. He stops in the doorway when he first sees his wife, and the emotional connection between them is so keenly apparent that the others are silent. Hale urges the men to leave the couple alone, which they do, but only after Danforth urges Proctor to confess.

The two are quiet as they look at each other in their dejected states, at the mercy of evil authority. Finally they touch and sit down, and Proctor first asks her about the baby she is carrying and about their other children. Elizabeth starts to weaken but stops herself, and he admits that he has been tortured and that his life will soon be over. He asks whether any of the others have confessed, and she says that a hundred or more have, but not those highly respected people such as Rebecca. He asks specifically about Giles Corey, and his wife relates the cruel, inhuman death he suffered. Corey would plead neither guilty—for he did not want to lie—nor not guilty in court, because if he pleaded not guilty they could hang him and auction his property; since Corey would not plead, his property would rightfully be left to his sons. But the court was not about to be outsmarted by Corey; they tortured him by placing large stones on his body, believing they could force him to plead. Still Corey would not give in, and so he died from being crushed.

Even after hearing about these instances of courage, Proctor tells his wife he has been thinking of confessing, but then he immediately asks her what she thinks of this decision. Elizabeth says she cannot judge him, and she says he must do what he thinks is right. She then says she wants him to live. Proctor explains his reason for confessing. He sees that it is the most upright people who are determined not to confess and says that he does not fit in this category; it is a pretense for him to be a part of this group, he says. God sees him for the man that he is already, and this confession will not change that perspective. He still asks his wife's opinion after giving this explanation.

Elizabeth warns him that her forgiveness means nothing if he cannot forgive himself. Now he is in agony over the decision, but she tells him that whatever choice he makes she knows that he is a good man. She then starts to admit her own sins, telling him that by being a cold wife she encouraged his cheating. He interrupts, not wanting her to take on any guilt, but she continues. She says that he has had to take on her sins, and she reveals that all along she had such a low opinion of herself that she could not believe that anyone would love her; she lived constantly in suspicion, cold and unable to express her love to him.

Before Proctor can respond, the couple is interrupted by Hathorne, who asks what Proctor has decided, telling them that the sun is almost up and the deadline imminent. Elizabeth again tells her husband he must do what he wishes, and he turns from her to Hathorne and in a hollow voice tells him he wants his life. Hathorne asks him if this means he will confess, and Proctor repeats that he wants his life. This is a good enough answer for Hathorne, who runs off with joy, yelling down the hallway. Proctor and Elizabeth are left alone again for just a few moments, and Proctor says he knows Elizabeth would never confess. "You would not; if tongs of fire were singeing you you would not! It is evil. Good, then—it is evil, and I do it!"

Danforth enters with Parris, Hale, and Cheever, and Cheever prepares to take Proctor's statement. Proctor questions why it must be written and is told that the statement will be posted on the church door. Danforth starts questioning Proctor, who is not quick to answer, and Danforth tries to rush him by reminding him that the sun is lighting the sky and people are waiting at the scaffold. Proctor begins to answer Danforth's questions, and Rebecca Nurse is brought in, also seriously deteriorated, needing help to walk. She is happy to see Proctor, but he turns away from her. Danforth tells Rebecca to take heed of Proctor's example, and as he starts to question him again, Rebecca realizes what is happening and calls out to Proctor, astonished. He stays facing the wall and, speaking through his teeth, continues to answer Danforth.

Danforth asks Rebecca if she will confess, and instead of answering him she again calls out, "Oh, John—God send his mercy on you!" Persisting, Danforth asks if she will confess, and she says she cannot since it is a lie. Danforth focuses again on Proctor, this time asking if he has seen Rebecca in the company of the devil. Proctor must be prompted again to answer, and quietly he says he has not. Danforth realizes he may not get the full confession he had envisioned, since each time he asks Proctor if he has seen a particular person with the devil, Proctor answers that he has not. Danforth warns, "I am not empowered to trade your life for a lie. You have most certainly seen some person with the devil." Speaking of those soon to be hanged, Proctor responds: "They think to go like saints. I like not to spoil their names." Danforth is astonished and asks again who he saw with the devil, but Proctor will not give him a name.

Hale and Parris are fearful as they see the questioning turn sour. They urge Danforth to be satisfied with what Proctor has agreed to, and the deputy governor gives in and tells Cheever to give the statement to Proctor to sign. Proctor looks at it and says it is enough that they have witnessed his confession. But Danforth will not relent on this point. Proctor struggles but then signs the paper, and Parris calls out praise to God. But Proctor, apparently still in turmoil and now with a raging anger building inside him, takes the paper back as Danforth reaches for it. Proctor tells the men that they have seen him sign it and it does not need to be made public. He says that he will not allow them to use him and that it will blacken all of his jailed friends if his statement is nailed to the church door on the very day of their executions.

Danforth says he must have the written statement, to which Proctor replies that the court's word should be good enough without the paper. Suspicious now, Danforth asks him whether it is the same if he gives up the paper or not, and Proctor cries out that it is not the same. Danforth asks if he plans to deny the confession when he leaves, but Proctor replies that he will not and cries out: "Because it is my name! . . . Because I lie and sign myself to lies! Because I am not worth the dust on the feet of them that hang!" With this, Danforth tells him that if the confession is a lie he cannot accept it. Proctor does not reply. Danforth asks him again if the paper is a lie. In response Proctor rips it and crumples it; his breast is heaving, and he weeps in rage.

Danforth calls for the marshal to take Proctor away, as both Parris and Hale yell to Proctor that he cannot destroy the confession. Full of tears, Proctor tells them, "I can. And there's your first marvel, that I can. You have made your magic now, for now I do think I see some shred of goodness in John Proctor. Not enough to weave a banner with, but white enough to keep it from such dogs." He is happy to not give the men what they want and now apparently is at peace with his decision. As his wife runs to him and cries, he advises, "Give them no tear! Tears pleasure them! Show honor now; show a stony heart and sink them with it!" He lifts Elizabeth and kisses her passionately, apparently now feeling free.

Rebecca yells that he has nothing to fear, while Danforth shouts for them all to be hanged. Rebecca stumbles, nearly collapsing as she is led away. We wonder if this struggle has been too much for her. Parris, still fearing the town will turn on him, begs Elizabeth to convince Proctor to confess. Drumrolls are heard outside. Hale, too, pleads for Elizabeth to talk sense into her husband, again arguing that Proctor's action is one of pride and that there will be no benefit from his death. Elizabeth, "supporting herself against collapse," cries, "He have his goodness now. God forbid I take it from him!" There is a final drumroll crash. Hale cries and prays frantically. The sunrise is shining on Elizabeth's face as the drums continue to rattle and the curtain falls.

Directly following the printed play, there are notes from Miller that reveal what happened to some of the actual people who appeared as characters in his play "not long after the fever died." Parris was voted out of his position and left town. Legend says that Abigail became a prostitute in Boston. Elizabeth Proctor remarried four years after her husband's death.

Then twenty years after the last execution, the government gave money to living victims and to the families of those who had been killed. Yet wickedness still surrounded the affair, since some money was given to those who had been informers at the trials as well. In March 1712 the congregation rescinded excommunications, following the orders of the government. Some farms of victims became ruined, with no one wanting to buy them for more than a century. "To all intents and purposes, the power of theocracy in Massachusetts was broken," Miller writes.

John Hale Makes "A Modest Enquiry into the Nature of Witchcraft" (1702)

Here was generally acknowledged to be an error (at least on the one hand) but the Querie is, Wherein?

[A.] 1. I have heard it said, That the Presidents [Precedents] in England were not so exactly followed, because in those there had been previous quarrels and threatnings of the Afflicted by those that were Condemned for Witchcraft; but here, say they, not so. To which I answer.

1. In many of these cases there had been antecedent personal quarrels, and so occasions of revenge; for some of those Condemned, had been suspected by their Neighbours several years, because after quarrelling with their Neighbours, evils had befallen those Neighbours. As may be seen in the Printed Tryals of S.M. and B.B. [Susannah Martin and Bridget Bishop] and others. And there were other like Cases not Printed.

2. Several confessors acknowledged they engaged in the quarrels of other their confederates to afflict persons. As one Timothy Swan suffered great things by Witchcrafts, as he supposed and testified. And several of the confessors said they did so torment him for the sake of one of their partners who had some offence offer'd her by the said Swan. And others owned they did the like in the behalf of some of their confederates.

3. There were others that confessed their fellowship in these works of darkness, was to destroy the Church of God (as above in part rehearsed) which is a greater piece of revenge then to be avenged upon one particular person.

[A.] 2. It may be queried then, How doth it appear that there was a going too far in this affair.

1. By the numbers of the persons accused which at length increased to about an hundred and it cannot be imagined that in a place of so much knowledge, so many in so small a

compass of Land should so abominably leap into the Devils lap at once.

2. The quality of several of the accused was such as did bespeak better things, and things that accompany salvation. Persons whose blameless and holy lives before did testify for them. Person that had taken greater pains to bring up their Children in the nurture and admonition of the Lord: Such as we had Charity for, as for our own Souls: and Charity is a Christian duty commended to us: 1. Cor. 13 Chapt., Col. 3.14, and in many other Scriptures.

3. The number of the afflicted by Satan dayly increased, till about Fifty persons were thus vexed by the Devil. This gave just ground to suspect some mistake, which gave advantage to the accuser of the Brethren [Satan] to make a breach upon us.

4. It was considerable that Nineteen were Executed, and all denied the Crime to the Death, and some of them were knowing persons, and had before this been accounted blameless livers. And it is not to be imagined, but that if all had been guilty, some would have had so much tenderness as to seek Mercy for their Souls in the way of Confession and sorrow for such a Sin. And as for the condemned confessors at the Bar (they being reprieved) we had no experience whether they would stand to their Self-condemning confessions, when they came to dye.

5. When this prosecution ceased, the Lord so chained up Satan, that the afflicted grew presently well. The accused are generally quiet, and for five years since, we have no such molestations by them.

6. It sways much with me that I have since heard and read of the like mistakes in other places. As in Suffolk in England about the year 1645 was such a prosecution, until they saw that unless they put a stop it would bring all into blood and confusion. The like hath been in France, till 900 were put to Death, And in some other places the like; So that N. England is not the only place circumvented by the wiles of the wicked and wisely Serpent in this kind. . . .

If there were an Error in the proceedings in other places, and in N. England, it must be in the principles proceeded upon in prosecuting the suspected, or in the misapplication of the principles made use of. Now as to the case of Salem, I conceive it proceeded from some mistaken principles made use of; for the evincing whereof, I shall instance some principles made use of here, and in other Countrys also, which I find defended by learned Authors writing upon that Subject.

ROBERT A. MARTIN CONSIDERS MILLER'S USE OF SALEM HISTORY IN *THE CRUCIBLE*

The events that eventually found their way into *The Crucible* are largely contained in the massive two volume record of the trials located in the Essex County Archives at Salem, Massachusetts, where Miller went to do his research. Although he has been careful to point out in a prefatory note that *The Crucible* is not history in the academic sense, a study of the play and its sources indicates that Miller did his research carefully and well. He found in the records of the trials at Salem that between June 10 and September 22, 1692, nineteen men and women and two dogs were hanged for witchcraft, and one man was pressed to death for standing mute. Before the affair ended, fifty-five people had confessed to being witches, and another hundred and fifty were in jail awaiting trial.

Focusing primarily upon the story of John Proctor, one of the nineteen who were hanged, Miller almost literally retells the story of a panic-stricken society that held a doctrinal belief in the existence of the Devil and the reality of witchcraft. The people of Salem did not, of course, invent a belief in witchcraft; they were, however, the inheritors of a witchcraft tradition that had a long and bloody history in their native England and throughout most of Europe. To the Puritans of Massachusetts, witchcraft was as real a manifestation of the Devil's efforts to overthrow "God's kingdom" as the periodic raids of his Indian disciples against the frontier settlements. . . .

In spite of an apparent abundance of historical material, the play did not become dramatically conceivable for Miller until he came upon "a single fact" concerning Abigail Williams, the niece of Reverend Parris:

> It was that Abigail Williams, the prime mover of the Salem hysteria, so far as the hysterical children were concerned, had a short time earlier been the house servant of the Proctors and now was crying out Elizabeth Proctor as a witch; but more—it was clear from the record that with entirely uncharacteristic fastidiousness she was refusing to include John Proctor, Elizabeth's husband, in her accusations despite the urgings of the prosecutors. Why? I searched the records of the trials in the courthouse at Salem but in no other instance could I find such a careful avoidance of the implicating stutter, the murderous, ambivalent answer to the sharp questions of the prosecutors. Only here, in Proctor's case, was there so clear an attempt to differentiate between a wife's culpability and a husband's.[10]

As in history, the play begins when the Reverend Samuel Parris begins to suspect that his daughter Betty has become ill because she and his niece Abigail Williams have "trafficked with spirits in the forest." The real danger Parris fears, however, is less from diabolical spirits than from the ruin that may fall upon him when his enemies learn that his daughter is suffering from the effects of witchcraft:

> *Parris.* There is a faction that is sworn to drive me from my pulpit. Do you understand that?
> *Abigail.* I think so, sir.
> *Parris.* Now then, in the midst of such disruption, my own household is discovered to be the very center of some obscene practice. Abominations are done in the forest—
> *Abigail.* It were sport, uncle![11]

As Miller relates at a later point in the play, Parris was a petty man who was historically in a state of continual bickering with his congregation over such matters as his salary, housing, and firewood. The irony of the above conversation in the play, however, is that while Parris is attempting to discover the "truth" to prevent it from damaging his already precarious reputation as Salem's minister, Abigail actually is telling him the historical truth when she says "it were sport." Whatever perverse motives may have subsequently prompted the adult citizens of Salem to cry "witch" upon their neighbors, the initiators of the Salem misfortune were young girls like Abigail Williams who began playing with spirits simply for the "sport" of it, as a release from an emotionally oppressive society. . . .

Miller's addition in *The Crucible* of an adulterous relationship between Abigail Williams and Proctor serves primarily as a dramatically imperative motive for Abigail's later charges of witchcraft against Elizabeth Proctor. Although it might appear that Miller is rewriting history for his own dramatic purposes by introducing a sexual relationship between Abigail and Proctor, his invention of the affair is psychologically and historically appropriate. As he makes clear in the prefatory note preceding the play, "dramatic purposes have sometimes required many characters to be fused into one; the number of girls . . . has been reduced; Abigail's age has been raised; . . ." Although Miller found that Abigail's refusal to testify against Proctor was the single historical dramatic "fact" he was looking for, there are two additional considerations that make adultery and Abigail's altered age plausible within the historical context of the events.

The first is that Mary Warren, in the play and in history, was simultaneously an accuser in court and a servant in Proctor's household. If an adulterous affair was probable, it would more likely have occurred between Mary Warren and Proctor than between Abigail Williams and Proctor; but it could easily have occurred. At the time, Mary Warren was a fairly mature young woman who would have had the features Miller has represented in Abigail: every emotional and sexual impulse, as well as the opportunity to be involved with Proctor. Historically, it was Mary Warren who attempted to stop the proceedings as early as April 19 by stating during her examination in court that the afflicted girls "did but dissemble": "Afterwards she started up, and said I will speak and cried out, Oh! I am sorry for it, I am sorry for it, and wringed her hands, and fell a little while into a fit again and then came to speak, but immediately her teeth were set, and then she fell into a violent fit and cried out, oh Lord help me! Oh Good Lord save me!"[13] As in the play, the rest of the girls prevailed by immediately falling into fits and spontaneously accusing her of witchcraft. As her testimony of April 21 and later indicates, however, she soon returned to the side of her fellow accusers. On June 30, she testified:

> The deposition of Mary Warren aged 20 years here testifieth. I have seen the apparition of John Proctor senior among the witches and he hath often tortured me by pinching me and biting me and choking me, and pressing me on my Stomach till the blood came out of my mouth and also I saw him torture Miss Pope and Mercy Lewis and John Indian upon the day of his examination and he hath also tempted me to write in his book, and to eat bread which he brought to me, which I refusing to do, John Proctor did most grievously torture me with a variety of tortures, almost Ready to kill me.[14]

Miller has reduced Mary Warren's lengthy and ambiguous trial testimony to four pages in the play by focusing on her difficulty in attempting to tell the truth after the proceedings were under way. The truth that Mary has to tell—"It were only sport in the beginning, sir"—is the same that Abigail tried to tell Parris earlier; but the telling has become compounded by the courtroom presence of Proctor, Parris, Hathorne and Danforth (two of the judges), the rest of the afflicted girls, and the spectators. In a scene taken directly from the trial records, Mary confesses that she and the other girls have been only pretending and that they have deceived the court. She has never seen the spirits or apparitions of the witches:

> *Hathorne.* How could you think you saw them unless you saw them?

Mary Warren. I—I cannot tell how, but I did. I—I heard the other girls screaming, and you, Your Honor, you seemed to believe them, and I—It were only sport in the beginning, sir, but then the whole world cried spirits, and I—I promise you, Mr. Danforth, I only thought I saw them but I did not.[15]

The second, additional consideration is that although Miller has raised Abigail's age from her actual eleven to seventeen, and has reduced the number of girls in the play to five only, such alterations for purposes of dramatic motivation and compression do not significantly affect the psychological or historical validity of the play. As the trial records clearly establish, individual and family hostilities played a large role in much of the damaging testimony given against those accused of witchcraft. Of the ten girls who were most directly involved in crying out against the witches, only three—Betty Parris (nine years old), Abigail Williams (eleven years), and Ann Putnam (twelve years) were below the age of sexual maturity. The rest were considerably older: Mary Walcott and Elizabeth Booth were both sixteen; Elizabeth Hubbard was seventeen; Susanna Sheldon was eighteen; Mercy Lewis was nineteen; Sara Churchill and Mary Warren (Proctor's servant) were twenty. In a time when marriage and motherhood were not uncommon at the age of fourteen, the hypothesis of repressed sexuality emerging disguised into the emotionally charged atmosphere of witchcraft and Calvinism does not seem unlikely; it seems, on the contrary, an inevitable supposition. . . .

On a larger scale, Miller brings together the forces of personal and social malfunction through the arrival of the Reverend John Hale, who appears, appropriately, in the midst of a bitter quarrel among Proctor, Parris, and Thomas Putnam over deeds and land boundaries. Hale, in life as in the play, had encountered witchcraft previously and was called to Salem to determine if the Devil was in fact responsible for the illness of the afflicted children. . . .

Hale's entrance at this particular point in the play is significant in that he interrupts an argument based on private and secular interests to bring "authority" to the question of witchcraft. His confidence in himself and his subsequent examination of the girls and Tituba (Parris's slave who inadvertently started the entire affair) represent and foreshadow the arrival of outside religious authority in the community. As an outsider who has come to weigh the evidence, Hale also helps to elevate the issue from a local to a regional level, and from an unofficial to an official theological inquiry. His heavy books of authority also symbolically anticipate the heavy authority of the judges who, as he will realize too late, are as susceptible to misinterpreting testimony based on spectral evidence as he is. . . .

The Reverend Hale is an extremely interesting figure historically, and following the trials he set down an account of his repentance entitled "A Modest Enquiry into the Nature of Witchcraft" (Boston, 1702). Although he was at first as overly zealous in his pursuit of witches as everyone else, very much as Miller has portrayed him in *The Crucible*, Hale began to be tormented by doubts early in the proceedings. His uncertainty concerning the reliability of the witnesses and their testimony was considerably heightened when his own wife was also accused of being a witch. Hale appears to have been as tortured spiritually and as dedicated to the "middle way" in his later life as Miller has portrayed him in *The Crucible*. Five years after Salem, he wrote in his "Enquiry":

> The middle way is commonly the way of truth. And if any can show me a better middle way than I have here laid down, I shall be ready to embrace it: But the conviction must not be by vinegar or drollery, but by strength of argument. . . . I have had a deep sence of the sad consequence of mistakes in matters Capital; and their impossibility of recovering when compleated. And what grief of heart it brings to a tender conscience, to have been unwittingly encouraging of the Sufferings of the innocent.[21]

Hale further commented that although he presently believed the executions to be the unfortunate result of human error, the

57

integrity of the court officials was unquestionable: "I observed in the prosecution of these affairs, that there was in the Justices, Judges and others concerned, a conscientious endeavour to do the thing that was right. And to that end they consulted the Presidents [Precedents] of former times and precepts laid down by Learned Writers about Witchcraft."[22] . . .

Largely through the Reverend Hale, Miller reflects the change that took place in Salem from an initial belief in the justice of the court to a suspicion that testimony based on spectral evidence was insufficient for execution. . . . By Act Three, however, Hale's confidence in the justice of the court has been badly shaken by the arrest and conviction of people like Rebecca Nurse who were highly respected members of the church and community. Hale, like his historical model, has discovered that "the whole green world" is burning indeed, and fears that he has helped to set the fire.

Partially as a result of Hale's preliminary investigation into the reality of Salem witchcraft, the Court of Oyer and Terminer was appointed to hear testimony and conduct the examinations. . . .

Like the rock at Salem, *The Crucible* has endured beyond the immediate events of its own time. If it was originally seen as a political allegory, it is presently seen by contemporary audiences almost entirely as a distinguished American play by an equally distinguished American playwright. As one of the most frequently produced plays in the American theater, *The Crucible* has attained a life of its own; one that both interprets and defines the cultural and historical background of American society. Given the general lack of plays in the American theater that have seriously undertaken to explore the meaning and significance of the American past in relation to the present, *The Crucible* stands virtually alone as a dramatically coherent rendition of one of the most terrifying chapters in American history.

Notes

10. Arthur Miller, *Arthur Miller's Collected Plays* (New York, 1957), p. 41; hereinafter cited as *C.P.* Present-day Salem is not where the witchcraft began in 1692. The town of Danvers, originally called

"Salem Village," is the location of Miller's play and the historical site in Essex County where the tragedy began. Danvers, or Salem Village, is a few miles northwest of present-day Salem, which was then called "Salem Town."

11. *C.P.*, p. 231.
13. Levin, *Salem*, p. 64.
14. Ibid., p. 61.
15. *C.P.*, pp. 302–306.
21. *Narratives of the Witchcraft Cases, 1648–1706*, ed. George Lincoln Burr (New York, 1914), pp. 404–405. Hale's account was written in 1697; published in 1702 after his death.
22. Ibid., p. 415.

SANTOSH K. BHATIA ON MILLER'S USE OF IRONY IN *THE CRUCIBLE*

Irony, which is an important aspect of tragedy, is used as a strong weapon in *The Crucible*. It is the most vitalizing force in the play which augments its tragic interest. In an interview with Henry Brandon, Miller once said, "A play is made by sensing how the forces in life simulate ignorance—you set free the concealed irony, the deadliest joke."[9] *The Crucible* it seems, is the best illustration of that statement. Irony is all pervasive in this play and contributes, in substantial measure, to its ultimate tragic impact. Irony, in tragedy, usually involves a tension between the statement and the meaning, appearance and reality, aspiration and achievement. In *The Crucible* it works both on the level of character and action. On the level of character its finest example is Proctor, who has the reputation of being the wisest and sanest of all the people in Salem, who fights in order to rescue others from injustice, but who commits the sin of adultery with Abigail which virtually sparks off the whole tragedy. In this . . . he resembles Oedipus who had the reputation of being the wisest and could solve the riddle of the sphinx and whom people always relied upon for help and guidance but who could not see that he actually bore the taint that plagued Thebes. Another character, besides Proctor, is Mr.

Hale, who comes as a learned theologist to Salem in order to rescue its people but ultimately ends up saying:

> I came into this village like a bridegroom to his beloved, bearing gifts of high religion; the very crowns of holy law I brought, and what I touched with my bright confidence, it died; and where I turned the eye of my great faith, blood flowed up. Beware, Goody Proctor—cleave to no faith when faith brings blood (p. 320).

Similarly, the irony of situation . . . can be seen at work throughout the play. The knowledge of the spectators is juxtaposed with the ignorance of the characters. Irony springs to surface when lies are extolled and believed in and the truth is brutally set aside. Theocracy becomes a farce and the wisdom of the churchmen mere folly. A pack of pretentious girls led by a vile and lascivious strumpet is able to deceive and hoodwink the entire wisdom of the court. The irony explodes the pretension of Tom Paine's statement that "in America the law is King."[10] Law proves a hollow myth. It is not merely the rigid enforcement of law but its wrong enforcement that results in a blatant miscarriage of justice. The law also fails to cope with the irrational forces at work in Salem and becomes an instrument of subversion. People are convicted and killed on such flimsy charges as are listed against Giles Corey's wife. Giles says:

> That bloody mongrel Walcott charge her. Y'see, he buy a pig of my wife four or five years ago, and the pig died soon after. So he came dancing in for his money back. So my Martha, she says to him, "Walcott, if you haven't the wit to feed a pig properly, you will not live to own many," she says. Now he goes to court and claims that from that day to this he cannot keep a pig alive for more than four weeks because my Martha bewitch them with her books! (p. 277).

Pigs and poppets serve as reasons good enough to accuse and arrest people. The stroke of irony, beneath all this is unmistakable. Jed Harris, one of the directors of the play, once pointed to the irony of situation involved in it: In Andover they hanged a dog. The dog said, "I'm not human" They said that is what you say and they hanged the dog.[11] The pungently ironic remark exposes the blind injustice at work in the world of *The Crucible*. The irony contained in the words of Danforth is also unmistakable:

> This is a sharp time, now, a precise time . . . we live no longer in the dusky afternoon when evil mixed itself with good and befuddled the world. Now, by God's grace, the shining sun is up (p. 293).

We as spectators know all the while of the gap that lies between Danforth's belief and the reality. We know that the time is not really sharp and bright and that they still live in the dusky afternoon when evil continues to befuddle the world by mixing itself with good; we also know that foul is fair and fair is foul. Its best example is found when Elizabeth tells Proctor how Abby is being venerated as a saint. She remarks:

> The town is gone Wild, I think . . . Abigail brings the other girls into the court, and where she walks the crowd will part like the sea for Israel. And folks are brought before them, and if they scream and howl and fall to the floor . . . the person's clapped in the jail for bewitching them (p. 263).

The suggested comparison between Abigail and Moses is a masterstroke of Miller's use of irony in this play. It reveals the extent to which evil is rampant in the world of *The Crucible*. Even the best of judges are deceived and confounded. They disbelieve what they see, and believe what they do not see. Note, for instance, the ironic sting in what Parris says, "We are here, Your Honor, Precisely to discover what no one has ever seen" (p. 300).

Irony is skillfully used in each successive scene of the play until the tragic tension mounts to its climax in Act III. The scene where Proctor brings Mary Warren to confess the truth is very crucial. She makes a deposition that she never saw any spirits and that they all had been pretending. But now that she is speaking the truth no one in the court accepts it. Proctor feels exasperated and, in a last bid to save his wife from Abby's false implications, he confesses lechery with Abby:

> Proctor (trembling, his life collapsing about him): I have known her, Sir, I have known her (p. 304).

Danforth can't believe what he says and asks Proctor: "You—You are a lecher?" Proctor replies: "A man will not cast away his good name. You surely know that." In a bid to expose Abby's vengeance, Proctor says:

> I have made a bell of my honor! I have rung the doom of my good name—you'll believe me Mr. Danforth! My wife is innocent except she knew a whore when she saw one! (p. 305).

The irony is again at work when a confirmation is sought from Elizabeth who, in Proctor's own words, "cannot lie." Danforth asks Proctor to turn his back and questions Elizabeth:

> Look at me! To your own knowledge, has John Proctor ever committed the crime of lechery? . . . Answer my question! Is your husband a lecher! (p. 307).

Without knowing that Proctor has already confessed, Elizabeth, in good faith, tells a lie and faintly says, "No, Sir." Like all the lies told by others before her, her lie is accepted as truth. Mr. Hale, who by now seems to serve as a veiled commentator on the action, says:

> Excellency, it is a natural lie to tell; I beg you stop now before another is condemned! I may shut my conscience to it no more—private vengeance is working through this testimony (p. 307).

The voice of reason is thus submerged and lost in an orgy of lies. Mary Warren, who gives testimony in favor of Proctor a minute ago, finding the balance going against him, shifts back and points at Proctor, "You're the Devil's man!" (p. 310). Proctor's faith in God is now completely shattered: "I say—I say—God is dead!" (p. 311). He laughs madly and says:

> A fire, a fire is burning! I hear the boot of Lucifer, I see his filthy face! And it is my face and yours Danforth! For them that quail to bring men out of ignorance, as I have quailed, and as you quail now when you know in all your black hearts that this be fraud—God damns our kind especially, and we will burn, we will burn together! (p. 311).

This frenzied speech not only reveals the agony of John Proctor, it also reminds us of those dark, mysterious, inscrutable forces which play a vital part in the tragic drama of human life. On the level of society these forces are represented by Danforth himself and the ecclesiastical court. The irrationality in their mode of working is referred to by Proctor when he says: "You are pulling Heaven down and raising up a whore!" (p. 311). . . .

The ultimate tragic irony is that Proctor is not convicted for the sin he actually commits and confesses openly in the court (i.e. adultery); he is executed for a sin he never commits, namely, witchcraft.

In its last analysis, *The Crucible* is a tragedy on the same pattern as Sophocles' *Antigone* and Shaw's *Saint Joan*. The dilemma facing Proctor is the same as faced by Joan, that is, should he or should he not save himself by confessing a liaison with evil? As in the case of Joan, the appeal of his character issues from a wonderful combination of courage and defenselessness. The trial scenes in both the plays are very gripping and disturbing. In the trial scene in *Saint Joan* "a young girl, alone, is seen and heard fighting for her life against the mightiest powers in the world."[12] The same is true of the trial scene in *The Crucible*, where a young man, dominated by reason and self-respect, is seen fighting with the irrational forces of society. In each case, the protagonist prefers death to a life without honor. Proctor's death sets a seal on his nobility and heroism. The title of the play also finds its true justification in

63

the end. The word "crucible" suggests a vessel which is used for heating and refining metals. Symbolically, it suggests a severe test for purification. For Proctor, the trial becomes a test by fire; his final execution suggests the purification of his spirit and its ultimate triumph. The title actually enshrines this victory.

Notes

9. "The State of the Theatre" (An Interview with Henry Brandon), *Harper's Magazine*, 221 (Nov. 1960), 64.

10. Quoted by Thomas E. Porter, *Myth and Modern American Drama* (1969; rpt. Ludhiana: Kalyani Publishers, 1971), p. 178.

11. Lewis Funke, "Thoughts on a Train Bound for Wilmington," *New York Times*, (January 18, 1953), Sec. II, p. 1.

12. A. C. Ward, ed., "Introduction," to *Saint Joan* (1954; Bombay: Orient Longman, 1964), p. 203.

ARTHUR MILLER DISCUSSES FIRST STEPS IN WRITING *THE CRUCIBLE*

I had known about the Salem witchcraft phenomenon since my American history class at Michigan, but it had remained in mind as one of those inexplicable mystifications of the long-dead past when people commonly believed that the spirit could leave the body, palpably and visibly. My mother might believe it still, if only in one corner of her mind, and I suspected that there were a lot of other people who, like me, were secretly open to suggestion. As though it had been ordained, a copy of Marion Starkey's book *The Devil in Massachusetts* fell into my hands, and the bizarre story came back as I have recalled it, but this time in remarkably well-organized detail.

At first I rejected the idea of a play on the subject. My own rationality was too strong, I thought, to really allow me to capture this wildly irrational outbreak. A drama cannot merely describe an emotion, it has to become that emotion. But gradually, over weeds, a living connection between myself and Salem, and between Salem and Washington, was made in my mind—for whatever else they might be, I saw that the House Un-American Activities Committee hearings in Washington were profoundly and even avowedly ritualistic. After all, in almost every case the Committee knew in advance what they wanted the witness to give them: the names of his comrades in the Party. The FBI had long since infiltrated the Party, and informers had long ago identified the participants in various meetings. The main point of the hearings, precisely as in seventeenth-century Salem, was that the accused make public confession, damn his confederates as well as his Devil master, and guarantee his sterling new allegiance by breaking disgusting old vows—whereupon he was let loose to rejoin the society of extremely decent people. In other words, the same spiritual nugget lay folded within both procedures—an act of contrition done not in solemn privacy but out in the public air. The Salem prosecution was actually on more solid legal ground since the defendant, if guilty of familiarity with the Unclean One, had broken a law against the practice of witchcraft, a civil as well as a religious offense; whereas the offender against HUAC could not be accused of any such violation but only of a spiritual crime, subservience to a political enemy's desires and ideology. He was summoned before the Committee to be called a bad name, but one that could destroy his career. . . .

Salem [back] then was a town dribbling away, half-forsaken. It was originally the salt lick of the mother colony of Plymouth to the south and had been bypassed by the modernization of industry a generation before. Lapped by the steely bay, it was dripping this afternoon in the cold black drizzle like some abandoned dog. I liked it, liked its morose and secret air. I went to the courthouse, asked the clerk for the town records for 1692, and had to wait a few minutes while he got out similar tomes for last year and three or four years earlier, handing them to a pair of real estate agents searching deeds for a property deal. The room was silent, and I found good gray light near a tall window that looked out over the water, or so I remember it now, the same hard silver water that the condemned must have beheld from the gallows on Witch Hill, of whose location no one is any longer sure. . . .

Like every criminal trial record, this one was filled with enticing but incomplete suggestions of relationships, so to speak, offstage. Next day in the dead silence of the little Historical Society building, two ancient lady guardians regarded me with steady gazes of submerged surprise; normally there were very few visitors. Here I found Charles W. Upham's quiet nineteenth-century masterpiece *Salem Witchcraft*, and in it, on my second afternoon, the hard evidence of what had become my play's center: the breakdown of the Proctor marriage and Abigail Williams's determination to get Elizabeth murdered so that she could have John, whom I deduced she had slept with while she was their house servant, before Elizabeth fired her.

" . . . During the examination of Elizabeth Proctor, Abigail Williams and Ann Putnam both made offer to strike at said Proctor; but, when Abigail's hand came near, it opened,—whereas it was made up into a fist before,—and came down exceeding lightly as it drew near to said Proctor, and at length, with open and extended fingers, touched Proctor's hood very lightly. Immediately, Abigail cried out her fingers, her fingers, her fingers burned. . . ."

The irony of this beautifully exact description is that its author was Reverend Parris, who was trying to show how real the girls' affliction was, and hence how dangerous people like Elizabeth Proctor could be. And irony, of course, is what is usually dispensed with, usually paralyzed, when fear enters the mind. Irony, indeed, is the supreme gift of peace. For it seemed obvious that Parris was describing a girl who had turned to look into her former mistress's face and experienced the joyous terror of the killer about to strike, and not only at the individual victim, the wife of a lover who was now trying to deny her, but at the whole society that was watching and applauding her valiant courage in ridding it of its pestilential sins. It was this ricocheting of the "cleansing" idea that drew me on day after day, this projection of one's own vileness onto others in order to wipe it out with their blood. As more than one private letter put it at the time, "Now no one is safe."

To make not a story but a drama of this parade of individual tragedies—this was the intimidating task before me, and I wondered if it would indeed be possible without diminishing what I had come to see as a veritable Bible of events. . . .

One day, after several hours of reading at the Historical Society, where it now seemed no one but I had ever entered to disturb the two gray guardians' expressionless tranquility, I got up to leave, and that was when I noticed hanging on a wall several framed etchings of the witchcraft trials, apparently made at the time by an artist who must have witnessed them. In one of them, a shaft of sepulchral light shoots down from a window high up in a vaulted room, falling upon the head of a judge whose face is blanched white, his long white beard hanging to his waist, arms raised in defensive horror as beneath him the covey of afflicted girls screams and claws at invisible tormentors. Dark and almost indistinguishable figures huddle on the periphery of the picture, but a few men can be made out, bearded like the judge, and shrinking back in pious outrage. Suddenly it became my memory of the dancing men in the synagogue on 114th Street as I had glimpsed them between my shielding fingers, the same chaos of bodily motion—in this picture, adults fleeing the sight of a supernatural event; in my memory, a happier but no less eerie circumstance—both scenes frighteningly attached to the long reins of God. I knew instantly what the connection was: the moral intensity of the Jews and the clan's defensiveness against pollution from outside the ranks. Yes, I understood Salem in that flash, it was suddenly my own inheritance. I might not yet be able to work a play's shape out of this roiling mass of stuff, but it belonged to me now, and I felt I could begin circling around the space where a structure of my own could conceivably rise.

I left Salem in the late afternoon, and the six o'clock news came on the radio with the black night like a cloak thrown over the windshield. The rain had not ceased. The announcer read a bulletin about Elia Kazan's testimony before the House Un-American Activities Committee and mentioned the people he had named, none of whom I knew. I had almost forgotten him by now, so deep had I been in the past. The announcer's voice seemed a violent, vulgar intrusion into a private anguish; I remember thinking that the issue was being made to sound altogether political when it was really becoming something else, something I could not name.

I was heading down toward New York, back into the world. A numbness held me. The bulletin was repeated again on the half-hour. I wished they would stop. I felt something like embarrassment, not only for him, but somehow for all of us who had shared the—comradeship, I suppose the word is, born of our particular kind of alienation. The political element was only a part of it, maybe even a small part. We had all cheered the same heroes, the same mythic resisters, maybe that was it, from way back in the Spanish war to the German antifascists and the Italians, brave men and women who were the best of our identity, those who had been the sacrifices of our time.

What we had now seemed a withering parody of what was being advertised as high drama. When the Committee knew all the names beforehand, there was hardly a conspiracy being unveiled but rather a symbolic display that would neither string anybody up on a gallows nor cause him to be cut down. No material thing had been moved one way or another by a single inch, only the air we all breathed had grown somewhat thinner and the destruction of meaning seemed total when the sundering of friendships was so often with people whom the witness had not ceased to love.

Approaching New York, I felt as always the nearness of the circumstantial, the bedrock real. As I headed downtown toward the Brooklyn Bridge on glistening wet roads, I found myself keeping to the slow side of the speedometer as though to protect what truth there was in me from skidding into oblivion. That I was committed to this play was no longer a question for me; I had made the decision without thinking about it somewhere between Salem and this city.

KAREN BOVARD LOOKS AT COMPETITION, SEXUALITY, AND POWER IN THE LIVES OF PURITAN WOMEN

Arthur Miller intended *The Crucible* to critique the witch-hunting mentality of McCarthyism and to expose a disturbing chapter in our colonial history: the Salem witch trials of 1692. It also invites analysis of gender roles, then and now, especially around the dynamics of girls in groups, competition among women for men's attention and for power, and problematic issues of sexual desire. Although John Proctor is unquestionably the play's protagonist, a rich array of female characters permits the exploration of women's behavior under the stresses of a rigid and repressive society.

Abigail Williams, the strikingly beautiful orphan who is the ringleader of a sizeable group of adolescent girls, propels the action. How the girls close ranks against outsiders, terrorize potential turncoats, and use hysteria to deflect doubts about their veracity provides a case study of peer group dynamics. Mary Warren's efforts to stand up to this cohort, and her eventual failure to do so, exposes some ways power can be wielded in groups. Do boys (and men) in groups behave similarly? Did McCarthy and his followers?

Abigail's natural leadership ability and boldness are attractive traits to the reader even as her absolute lack of moral scruples is repellent. It is her genius at manipulation which propels the girls from a position of powerlessness to the pinnacle of importance as "officials of the court" (60). This is a radical disruption of Salem's norms, where male ministers and judges hold all the seats of civic power.

Abigail's illegitimate desire for Proctor fuels her actions against innocent townspeople. Whether there is any desire that would be seen as legitimate for a girl in her position is a question worth raising. It is striking that there are no young male characters in the Salem of the play: only older married men. What's a girl to do, in the Salem of 1692? In Miller's play, fundamental frustrations (which are arguably worse for women than men, given the smaller range of social roles permitted to them) lead to slanderous and vindictive behaviors.

Miller mercilessly delineates the way Proctor's consummated desire for Abigail costs him deeply, both in the loss of his wife's trust and in self-loathing. Today's reader might ask about harassment since the affair begins when Abigail is in Proctor's employ and living under his roof. She is seventeen and he is in his thirties. There is no textual evidence that she resists his advances; rather, the contrary seems true. How do gender differences, as well as power and age variables, influence how we assign responsibility for sexual relationships?

Elizabeth, Proctor's wife, has her own complex relationship to desire. She understands Abigail sooner and better than does Proctor—"she wants me dead!" (61)—and tells him, "You have a faulty understanding of young girls. There is a promise made in any bed" (62). But she also comes to accept some responsibility for his straying: "It needs a cold wife to prompt lechery" (137). The very self-effacement Puritanism required of women robs Elizabeth of the ability to voice her own desire, even within the legitimacy of marriage: "I counted myself so plain, so poorly made, no honest love could come to me! Suspicion kissed you when I did; I never knew how I should say my love." (137).

Thwarted sexual desire is not the only kind Miller examines. Ann Putnam, embittered by the loss of seven children in childbirth, is among the first to level accusations of witchcraft at her neighbors. One of these is Rebecca Nurse, mother of eleven and grandmother of twenty-six, a figure renowned for integrity. The grief Ann Putnam feels at her thwarted motherhood is toxic, and she turns her resentment on Rebecca Nurse.

Basic to the events in the play is a profound puritanical mistrust of the body. It is the discovery that the girls have been dancing in the woods at night, perhaps naked, that precipitates the witch-hunt. Caught in scandalous behavior in a society that provides no outlet for exuberance, much less sexual exploration, several of the girls fall ill. Teachers might ask whether eating disorders today, or other related dysfunctions, could be similar last-ditch strategies for girls facing dilemmas to which they see no healthy solutions. Students of American history may want to consider what legacy our puritanical heritage has left in contemporary society around girls' struggles with desire and their bodies.

Presiding over the illicit gathering was Tituba, a slave from Barbados with knowledge of voodoo, whose "slave sense has warned her that, as always, trouble in this house eventually lands on her back" (8). Racial difference and Tituba's powerlessness make her the safest scapegoat for the disruptions—she is the first accused. Other differences mark early targets: The homeless Goody Good and mentally ill Goody Osburn are quickly named as witches. It has long been dangerous to be different in America, despite our rhetoric of inclusion. That far more women than men are accused and executed in Salem demonstrates that male privilege offers some protection from persecution: The more marginal one is—by race, gender, and class—the more vulnerable at times of social upheaval.

In addition to the McCarthy period, this play suggests study of witch trials during the Middle Ages and Renaissance in Europe, and raises questions about the gendered nature of that violence: Why were women so much more often accused of witchcraft than men, historically? Miller argues that the events in *The Crucible* are rooted in the demise of theocracy in New England (7, 146) and takes pains to document property disputes behind some of the accusations in Salem. That women could not *own* property but rather *were* property until relatively recently is fertile terrain for research. The play's title refers to an ordeal where one's true mettle is tested. Asking students to identify such moments in their own lives (or to interview parents and other adults about this) and compare lists of the events named by men and women may be revealing, as well.

ENOCH BRATER DISCUSSES THE PLAY'S HISTORICAL PARALLELS

It is *The Crucible*, Miller's most often produced play, that most significantly captures the climate of fear and the abuse of civil liberties set in motion by Senator Joseph McCarthy and other right-wing opportunists in the United States Congress. "I don't think I can adequately communicate the sheer density of the atmosphere of the time," Miller observed. "For the outrageous had so suddenly become the accepted norm." He told

Christopher Bigsby that "it was really a tremendous outburst of primitive human terror." . . . Although Miller would not be summoned before the House Committee on Un-American Activities (HUAC) for another three years, the play already displayed his disgust with Red-baiting, his contempt for those who named names and, above all, his clear-sightedness concerning the show-trial nature of the entire enterprise.

The progressive theater community in New York quickly became an early target for McCarthy and his henchmen. Liberal, urbane and Left-leaning, many of them members of the original Group Theatre with immigrant and often Eastern European Jewish roots (like Miller himself), the entertainment industry on both coasts provided some of the prime material HUAC needed to present its case before a provincial, puritanical and conservative America. Several members of the Group Theatre, for example, had indeed been members of the Communist Party in the 1930s, and all identified with the fight against poverty, inequality and fascism. Fifteen years later, in the first years of the Cold War, McCarthy knew "the heartland" well and how easily, especially in the dawning age of television, his Midwestern constituency as well as the truth could be manipulated. Those same live broadcasts of committee hearings would eventually prove his undoing, but in 1953 the stage was still his, as was a blacklist that stunted and in some cases ruined the careers of John Garfield, Phoebe Brand, Sam Wanamaker, Morris Carnovsky, Zero Mostel and Lee Grant. Others named names: Clifford Odets, Elia Kazan and, with a young family to feed and no visible means of support, the original Willy Loman himself, Lee J. Cobb. This was indeed, as Lillian Hellman called it, a "scoundrel time." Summoned to testify before the same committee about herself and her well-known relationship with Dashiell Hammett, she famously stood up and walked out of the chamber hearings, but not before announcing, theatrically, that she refused to cater her morality to "today's fashion." Miller's reaction to this lethal phase of McCarthyism was more muted, though it resulted in a major work for the American theater whose resonance would prove far more enduring.

In writing *The Crucible* Miller tried hard to avoid the strong emotional undertow that had an uncanny way of overwhelming the argumentative texture of works like *All My Sons* and especially *Death of a Salesman*. (Later he would admit that an audience must be made "to feel before it can be made to think.") Rather than situate the play in the contentious political climate of the McCarthyite present, he made the firm decision to look to the past not only for historical precedent but also for a controlling metaphor. "Gradually, over weeks," he wrote in *Timebends*, "a living connection between myself and Salem, and between Salem and Washington, was made in my mind—for whatever else they might be, I saw that the House Un-American Activities Committee hearings in Washington were profoundly and even avowedly ritualistic." Miller drove to the Atlantic coast of eastern Massachusetts to research letters, diaries and court records relating to the Salem witch trials of 1692, a murky period in New England history that resulted in the detention of more than 200 people. . . .

Salem's seventeenth-century victims refused to recant their confederacy with the forces of darkness; that was their crime and their undoing. What their judges required, as in the HUAC interrogations, was a "public confession," after which they could be "let loose to rejoin the society of extremely decent people." The Salem documents told the story the playwright had been looking for: "In effect, it came down to a government decree of *moral* guilt that could be easily made to disappear by ritual speech: intoning names of fellow sinners and recanting former beliefs." . . .

In 1996 Miller said he did not remember concentrating on the centrality of sexuality when he was working on the play: "I wasn't thinking in those terms, but that's an important element. The politically illicit always contains a germ of the sexually illicit." For Miller the play was about power "and the lust for it." He noticed, however, that almost every testimony he read in Salem "revealed the sexual theme"; the relief that came to those who testified "was orgasmic." The court even encouraged them to talk openly "about their sharing a bed with someone they weren't married to, a live human being now manacled before them courtesy of God's lieutenants." Guilt, the "guilt of illicit sexuality" had to be part of the public display. Only then could the sinner be returned to the fold. Repudiating suppressed feelings of hostility and alienation toward "standard daylight society as defined by its most orthodox proponents" would recertify and reinvigorate a threatened system of oppression— and those who held undisputed authority over it. That is why John Proctor becomes in the course of the play Miller's reluctant martyr. His refusal to tarnish his name, even in the face of certain death, is an ultimate and eloquent act of political dissent. "The longer I worked [on *The Crucible*]," Miller wrote, "the more certain I felt that as improbable as it might seem, there were moments when an individual conscience was all that could keep a world from falling." . . .

Not all of Miller's contemporaries bought the analogy *The Crucible* made between the Salem witch-hunt and the McCarthy show trials. The Communists were real, Frances Rudge (Kazan's third wife) protested, while the witches never existed. In the playwright's updating of what the Puritans called "the breaking of charity with one another" there was certainly no room for those who abhorred McCarthy's tactics but were equally horrified by the threat Stalin's outrages posed to the very idea of a liberal and humane democratic system. In a postscript to *Scoundrel Time* (1979) Lillian Hellman would have none of this: "I never want to live again to watch people turn into liars and cowards and others into frightened, silent collaborators. And to hell with the fancy reasons they give for what they did." In this regard the play has come to emblematize its period, both in its Cold War politics and pieties, but also in its passionate provocation. Danforth, moreover, as the play's chief interrogator, delivers a pivotal speech so full of menace that it is absolutely chilling in its contemporary implications: "You must understand, sir, a person is either with this Court or against it; there be no road between. This is a new time, a precise time; we live no longer in the dusky afternoon when evil mixed itself with good and befuddled the world. Now, by God's grace, the good folk and the evil entirely separate! I hope you will find your place with us." The great strength of a play like *The Crucible* is the way it liberates its audience from the merely literal. Any threat to entrenched authority at the moment when society is in transition, as Salem surely is in Miller's play, will find its scapegoats. This quintessentially American play does so tellingly, by casting "black magic" in the form of the predictably dark-skinned Tituba, the slave who was born in Barbados. In this monumental work Miller shows us that the outsider we fear most lies hidden deep within ourselves. The greatest threat of all is our ability to be so easily seduced not by the Devil, but by the lure of power in the crucible of tyranny: one of Proctor's principal accusers merely wants his land. "The artist's powerful desire," Miller wrote, "to penetrate life's chaos, to make it meaningfully cohere, has literally created a truth as substantial as a sword for later generations to wield against their own oppression."

STEVEN R. CENTOLA EXAMINES THE POSSIBILITY FOR HUMAN REDEMPTION IN THE PURITAN COMMUNITY

Miller's [*Death of a Salesman*] gives us an unblinking look at the terrifying darkness that lies coiled within existence. Attendant to this dark vision is the discovery that the light enkindled by human kindness and love can give human life a brilliance and luster that will never be extinguished. Willy dies, but death does not defeat Willy Loman; as the Requiem demonstrates, Willy will continue to live on in the memories and lives of others. Through his remarkable fusion of opposites that express both the form and the vision of the play, Miller reveals the condition of tension that is life and human existence. Because of its perfect integration of form, character, and action, *Death of a Salesman* is a modern masterpiece that celebrates, as Chris Bigsby eloquently states, "the miracle of human life, in all its bewilderments, its betrayals, its denials, but, finally, and most significantly, its transcendent worth" ("Poet" 723).

"*The Crucible*," writes Miller, "is, internally, *Salesman's* blood brother. It is examining the questions I was absorbed with before—the conflict between a man's raw deeds and his conception of himself, the question of whether conscience is in fact an organic part of the human being, and what happens when it is handed over not merely to the state or the mores of the time but to one's friend or wife" ("Brewed in *The Crucible*," *Theater Essays* 172–173). The powerful manner in which *The Crucible* explores these questions explains why it is also regarded as a masterpiece of the modern stage. *The Crucible* is Arthur Miller's most frequently produced play and speaks to people all over the world of the need to resist tyranny and oppression. Miller's play transcends cultural and geographical boundaries with its inspired depiction of one man's heroic struggle to preserve his honor when threatened by a corrupt state authority. With its intense dramatic action and its absorbing look at the debilitating effects of guilt, fear, repression, personal betrayal, mass hysteria, and public confession, *The Crucible* shows how an individual can rise above the conditions surrounding him and transform guilt into responsibility and thereby defeat the deterministic forces, both within and outside him, that threaten to destroy his identity as well as his humanity.

The Crucible dramatizes one of the darkest episodes in American history: the Salem Witch Trials of 1692. Making just a few alterations to the historical record in the interest of intensifying the play's dramatic action and clarifying and revealing the characters' hidden motivation, Miller shows what happens when girls in the repressive Puritan community of Salem Village in 1692 make unfounded accusations of witchcraft against their neighbors. Hundreds are arrested and convicted of witchcraft and nineteen innocent people are hanged. Among those incarcerated is John Proctor, a citizen of the community, a successful farmer and landowner who has committed adultery with Abigail Williams, one of the principal accusers and witnesses for the state. Proctor's guilt over his infidelity and conviction that he is a sinner, and therefore not like the falsely accused, temporarily cause him to sign a phony confession of witchcraft in an effort to save his life and protect his family. But when he realizes that his confession must be made public and therefore will be used to damage the credibility of his friends and neighbors and justify their persecution, Proctor fiercely denounces the court and tears up his confession. In a powerful dramatic scene, Proctor insists that his name not be used to damage the reputation of others, and even though his inspiring act of courage and nobility leads directly to his execution, it simultaneously becomes the basis for his own personal redemption.

Ironically, because of Proctor's defiant act of heroism and decision to die a noble death rather than live ignobly, it is easier to see how *The Crucible* demonstrates the possibility for human transcendence than is at first evident in both *All My Sons* and *Death of a Salesman*. Yet the conditions for such individualistic behavior are certainly far less favorable in the Puritan community of 1692 that Miller dramatizes in *The Crucible* than in the American society of the 1940s he depicts in *All My Sons* and *Death of a Salesman*. Because Salem Village was a theocracy, every facet of an individual's life in that community could arguably be seen as demonstrating the inevitable intersection of the societal and personal dimensions of a person's experience. In essence, everything a person said or did in Salem Village in 1692 could have been construed as having a direct bearing on society and, therefore, would unquestionably receive the close scrutiny of the larger community. Yet, in spite of the strong limitations and constraints placed on an individual's personal liberties and freedoms in that society, John Proctor is able to rise above the deterministic conditions surrounding him and find the courage and strength needed to denounce the court's inane proceedings. Through the crucible of his personal suffering, Proctor embraces values that are life-affirming, and with his acceptance of his personal responsibility for the welfare of others, Proctor defeats death and wins a victory for humankind.

D. QUENTIN MILLER ON GOOD VERSUS EVIL, BLACK VERSUS WHITE, AND RELIGION VERSUS WITCHCRAFT

The history of witchcraft in *The Crucible* is a struggle between wrong and right; the history of McCarthyism is a struggle between left and right; but the history that is obscured by both of these other histories is the struggle between black and white. Ironically, David Levin quotes Miller as describing the play as "an attack on black-or-white thinking",[17] referring to dualistic thinking while evoking race unconsciously. Christopher Bigsby similarly quotes Miller as describing the "extreme view of the world" held by the 1692 Salemites this way: "Because they are white, opposition is completely black."[18]

The link between blackness and evil in the play, melded in the furnace of language, is forged through the evocation of voodoo. American audiences of the mid-twentieth century would undoubtedly scoff at witchcraft as something of which only a seventeenth-century Puritan would be frightened. Miller even says, with an enlightened twentieth-century chuckle, "There was a fundamental absurdity in the Salem witch-hunt, of course, since witches don't exist."[19] In the same essay he writes, alluding to McCarthyist censorship, "By 1950 or thereabouts there were subjects one would do better to avoid and even words that were best left unspoken."[20] Although Miller is talking about communism, one of those words, apparently, was "voodoo", which lingers in the play's margins like Tituba herself. Miller's audiences would likely agree with him that "witches don't exist", but they were also aware that at least one form of "black magic" was very much in the air at the time of the play's first production. Hansen writes that one of the two "dramatic reasons" Miller has "for blackening Tituba . . . is to dramatize her as a voodoo priestess".[21] This plausibly explains why some nineteenth- and twentieth-century writers possibly altered Tituba's ethnic heritage from Arawak to African, but Hansen doesn't explore its complexities: what is dramatic about a voodoo priestess? Before answering that question directly, I wish to turn to the section of the play where "voodoo" is evident, but unnamed as such, for the word "voodoo" was not a part of the English language during the time of the Salem witch trials.[22] By 1953, though, it was a common and commonly misconstrued concept in American culture, and it had a long history on the page, the stage and the screen.

Witchcraft has its roots in Europe; voodoo (and all of its variants) has its roots in the Caribbean, presumably as a syncretic response to African religious beliefs in contact with the dominant Christianity of the Europeans who imported slaves. The contemporary audience is frightened of Tituba because, on some level, it suspects that her voodoo—whether playful or serious—is a powerful, subversive force in American culture, much worse than Proctor's lust because much less familiar. American culture circa 1953 associates voodoo with the minority other: immigrants, blacks, non-Christians, and speakers of imperfect English, all of which are represented by Tituba. In its most general sense, witchcraft saw its demise in America at the end of the seventeenth century; but voodoo, witchcraft's Africanist alter-ego, is a twentieth-century phenomenon (insofar as it affects the American imagination) which had become a vivid part of popular culture when *The Crucible* was first produced. Although twentieth-century Americans did not take voodoo seriously in the way seventeenth-century New Englanders took witchcraft seriously, voodoo signifies a persistent American mistrust and misunderstanding of non-European cultural traditions. This misunderstanding, no less than Proctor's adultery, Abigail's vengeance, Danforth's pride in his reputation, the young girls' collective fear of persecution, or Parris' weak egotism, is a primary reason why innocent people are executed in Miller's fictional rendering of history.

Voodoo is framed in American culture as a kind of horror, imported from the poorest country in the Western hemisphere to the wealthiest. Voodoo in American popular thought is regarded with both a wary respect for the power of belief systems of African origin and an association between those systems and their threats to American identity: irrationality, poverty and revenge against the powerful. The characters in Miller's play turn the common American perception of voodoo into an anxious semiotic debate when they encounter a doll ("poppet") in the Proctor household. When Cheever discovers the doll that Mary has given to his wife Elizabeth, Proctor asks, "What signifies a poppet?"

CHEEVER: Why, a poppet—*he gingerly turns the poppet over*—a poppet may signify—Now, woman, will you please to come with me?
. . .

HALE: What signifies a poppet, Mr. Cheever?
CHEEVER, *turning the poppet over in his hands*: Why, they say it may signify that she—*He has lifted the poppet's skirt, and his eyes widen in astonished fear*. Why, this, this—
PROCTOR, *reaching for the poppet*: What's there?
CHEEVER: Why—*he draws out a long needle from the poppet*—it is a needle! Herrick, Herrick, it is a needle! *Herrick comes toward him*.
PROCTOR, *angrily, bewildered*: And what signifies a needle!
CHEEVER, *his hands shaking*: Why, this go hard with her, Proctor, this—I had my doubts, Proctor, I had my doubts, but here's calamity. *To Hale, showing the needle*: You see it, sir, it is a needle!
HALE: Why? What meanin' has it? (*C* 70)

The audience does not share Proctor's and Hale's ignorance about dolls and needles: it is keenly aware that someone suffers bodily pain when a pin is stuck in a homemade doll. Yet the fact that a discussion of voodoo is so carefully avoided in this crucial exchange, even as the doll and needle are interpreted as "hard proof" (*C* 71), reveals the play's persistent unwillingness to look at Tituba and her supposed practices directly. She is out of our sight and her conjuring is judiciously unnamed: Cheever fairly stutters his lines, skipping over all mention of voodoo and declining to interpret the significance of a needle in a doll.

Tituba has nothing to do with the poppet, of course; Mary has placed it in the Proctor household at Abigail's urging to frame Elizabeth. As the representative of Afro-Caribbean culture, and as one who has already confessed, Tituba is implicated here; yet Abigail has again used the power of widespread suspicion of Tituba's beliefs to her own advantage. The actual incidents that precipitated the Salem witch trials were the baking of a witch-cake and the attempt to divine the future through reading an egg white dropped into a glass of water. These were practices of English origin.[23] David Hall argues that a wide variety of "magical" practices coexisted with Christianity in seventeenth-century New England: "Some people practiced magic to defend themselves from witchcraft, and some consulted fortune-tellers."[24] Although *maleficium*—magical practices involving malicious or evil intent—also might have involved "a model of clay or puppet stuck with pins", this type of "witchcraft" was not part of the Salem witch trials:

> What is very clear from the record of the Salem events is the total lack of proof that at Tituba's instigation the girls ran naked through the woods, drank blood, danced to drums, or stuck pins in waxen images. Or even that the girls had done so without her assistance. These are fictional creations of other eras and not part of the seventeenth-century record of events.[25]

The contemporary audience of *The Crucible* associates pin-stuck "poppets" with voodoo dolls and sees Tituba behind them even though she is clearly not involved in the placement of this one. In this case Abigail does not even have to point her finger at Tituba or act baffled that "she spoke Barbados" to ascribe guilt to her. Miller substitutes a symbol of "voodoo" that the audience would understand for one of the practices that actually took place in Salem in 1692 (the witch-cake and divination practices).

"Voodoo" is American shorthand for any number of African-influenced "superstitions" practiced in the Caribbean resulting in a unique brand of occultist kitsch. . . .

In Barbados, Tituba's country of origin, obeah exists but is eclipsed by "official" (mainly Christian) religions. Barbados is believed to have the highest concentration of churches in the world, and obeah, suppressed early on by British colonial rulers, is a felony.

In the United States, "voodoo" has become the word to signify all of these practices because of the proximity of Haiti to the United States, the influence of Haitian immigrants on the popular tourist destination of New Orleans (as well as Brooklyn, where Miller spent his adolescence), and especially the occupation of Haiti by US Marines from 1915 to 1934. . . .

Once the poppet surfaces in Act II as evidence, Tituba's guilt is established through the audience's associations based on popular culture's saturation with voodoo. She disappears for much of the remainder of the play. Her reappearance at the beginning of Act IV is preceded by the following stage directions describing the Salem jail cell: "*The place is in darkness but for the moonlight seeping through the bars. It appears empty*" (*C* 112). The jail cell that "appears empty" contains Tituba and her mad, accused cellmate, Sarah Good. The dark cell's empty appearance underscores the undeniable link between blackness and invisibility. Tituba is briefly conjured out of the darkness before disappearing from the play altogether. The jailer does not even acknowledge her presence in the empty-appearing cell; he calls for Sarah only (*C* 112). Tituba remains out of our sight as long as possible in the drama; she is ultimately more victim than villain. Abigail Williams invokes a greater degree of terror than Tituba does, but Tituba embodies much of the guilt and shame that is the other side of Proctor's honor. She lurks in the shadows of the play, largely invisible, but somehow unsettling to its outcome. . . .

If one is concerned with the historical probability that Tituba was an Arawak Indian, it could be argued that the Native presence in the play, like the Africanist presence, is similarly demonized, unseen and co-opted. If Christopher Bigsby is right when he asserts that "*The Crucible* is perhaps about the tendency—never fully resisted—to condemn difference,"[36] then it follows that the two oppressed racial minorities of early American history are collapsed in one character in Miller's play. Abigail attributes her own ruthless behavior and lack of fear to the brutality of Indians towards her family; she threatens Betty by pointing out, "I saw Indians smash my dear parents' heads on the pillow next to mine, and I have seen some reddish work done at night, and I can make you wish you had never seen the sun go down!"

(*C* 19). The "reddish" work of Indians—the bloody revenge of massacres—lodges in a white child's psyche to create in her a cool, exacting brutality that enables her to lie in court, to threaten her friends and her lover, to send dozens of accused witches to the gallows, and finally to steal from her uncle and escape unscathed. But an Indian slave was perhaps too abstract and unfamiliar a figure for Miller's audience to comprehend. The "black magic" of African origin is similarly available to Abigail's mind: it empowers her to lead her friends into the forbidden underside of white, Christian, American experience: nakedness, dancing, music (Barbados songs), eating and drinking some intoxicating brew. Abigail, the powerful white co-opter of subaltern cultures, has grown stronger from her contact with Native American and African American others, and she is *never punished* for her crime. Tituba, on the other hand, practices the beliefs of her native land at the bidding of a white relative of her master, and she is imprisoned as a result.

Notes

17. D. Levin, *In Defense of Historical Literature: Essays on American History, Autobiography, Drama, and Fiction* (New York, 1967), pp. 90–92.

18. Bigsby, *Arthur Miller*, p. 158.

19. Miller, *Echoes*, p. 284.

20. Ibid., p. 278.

21. Hansen, "The Metamorphosis of Tituba", p. 10. See also Breslaw, *Tituba, Reluctant Witch*, p. xxi.

22. The *Oxford English Dictionary* lists the first appearances of the word "voodoo" in English around 1880.

23. Breslaw, *Tituba, Reluctant Witch*, p. 90. Ann Petry's *Tituba of Salem Village* (New York, 1964) preserves the witch-cake incident, but gives some credence to Tituba's powers as a clairvoyant (as well as to Bette Parris') as she has them staring repeatedly into glasses of water that tell them the future. Also, Petry has Tituba reading Tarot cards to divine the future, a practice originating in Europe. There is a minor episode with a corn husk doll thrown into a fire in Petry's novel, but Tituba is not involved.

24. Hall, *Worlds of Wonder*, p. 7.

25. Breslaw, *Tituba, Reluctant Witch*, pp. 91–2.

36. Bigsby, *Arthur Miller*, p. 164.

The women characters in my plays are very complex. They've been played somewhat sentimentally, but that isn't the way they were intended. There is a more sinister side to the women characters in my plays. These women are of necessity auxiliaries to the action, which is carried by the male characters. But they both receive the benefits of the male's mistakes and protect his mistakes in crazy ways. They are forced to do that. So the females are victims as well.

     —Arthur Miller, 1985, Roudané, "Interview"

. . . Miller sexualizes his women, and if they are neither wives nor potential wives, they are illicit playmates: other men's partners ripe for seduction, harlots on call, or temptresses offering the thrill of danger. When a man assesses a woman, he sees first her sexual potential. . . .

The youngest of Miller's transgressive women is Abigail, and even before she speaks, Miller remarks on her "endless capacity for dissembling"; that is, she is an actress, a deceiver whose manner and behavior others trust at their peril (230). Such a person is dangerous, for not only is *The Crucible* at one level a courtroom drama, Miller's Salem moves according to courtroom procedure, and the most important discourse is composed of confession and testimony, both scrutinized for veracity and credibility. In a town where people seek to rely on what others say, someone who can lie with a straight face not only has the potential to escape the consequences of her actions, she can touch others at their points of greatest vulnerability. She not only deceives and conceals her intentions, she simulates; that is, she is able to become what she is not in order to put others at a disadvantage and gain the upper hand. . . .

The play traces Abigail's rise to become a force in the community. In the first act, alone with the girls, Abigail engages in damage control, trying to arouse Betty and setting strict limits on what the others may tell the adults. She is ruthless.

> Now look you. All of you. We danced. And Tituba conjured Ruth Putnam's dead sisters. And that is all. And mark this. Let either of you breathe a word, or the edge of a word, about the other things, and I will come to you in the black of some terrible night and I will bring a pointy reckoning that will shudder you. And you know I can do it; I saw Indians smash my dear parents' heads on the pillow next to mine, and I have seen some reddish work done at night, and I can make you wish you had never seen the sun go down! (238)

She offers no leeway, no compromise; either they will keep counsel perfectly or she will punish them with agony and fear. In this little community, this society of girls, Abigail is a tyrant who rules by terror and threat. Mercy is a willing conspirator—"merciless," as Miller would have it—who picks up Abigail's cue to bully and intimidate Mary, who shrinks from them both. Yet all are Abigail's subordinates, and she seeks to control the adults as well. Elizabeth relates Mary's version of her new status: "She speak of Abigail, and I thought she were a saint, to hear her. Abigail brings the other girls into the court, and where she walks the crowd will part like the sea for Israel" (263). John realizes that she is no longer the girl he thought he could dismiss, and all tread with care where Abigail is concerned. . . .

Abigail plays Proctor more delicately than any of the others. She tells him he's strong and that she waits for him every night, and he gives her some of what she wants—a smile and a bit of banter. Yet when he won't fully cooperate, she reminds him of how her very presence affects him: he "sweated like a stallion" whenever she came near, and even now, his heat draws her to the window, where she sees him looking up, "burning in your loneliness" (240–41). The images of heat and especially of perspiration raise the stakes; she so affects him that he cannot control himself, his sweating noticeable even for a farmer, a man who surely perspires heavily in the normal course of a day's work, especially on the warm, muggy days of a Massachusetts spring. Abigail presents herself as a "wild thing," an exciting alternative to a woman she's already branded as cold. She even makes herself weak and vulnerable for him, weeping, clutching him, and protesting her helplessness in the face of her obsession with him. She offers the compliment of captivation. Proctor believes her performance, but Miller's warning—that she dissembles endlessly—suggests the possibility that she is, as ever, playing a role.

Proctor, the man who insists on exposing deceit, who suffers in his own hypocrisy, and who would master the situation that enfolds Salem, cannot manage his erotic fascination with Abigail. Their sexual relationship colors every word they exchange; she because she cannot give up the hope of his return, and he because he cannot shed his desire for her. In spite of his determination, Proctor cannot help admitting, "I may have looked up" (241). Elizabeth understands her husband's danger, explaining that the risk lies less in what Abigail might betray about Proctor than in the girl's conviction that the farmer cannot resist her. She warns him, "There is a promise made in any bed," for she realizes, as he does not just yet, that by having sexual relations with the girl, he has placed his credit in her hands and compromised his safety. She knows that the connection is stronger and more powerful than he is willing to admit, that they were more than stallion and mare and that "she has an arrow in you yet" (271). She advises him to "go and tell her she's a whore. Whatever promise she may sense—break it, John, break it" (270). The stakes are high; only if John risks his reputation will he have a chance to free himself. . . .

Proctor is an active man in his middle thirties, and by matching him with the "strikingly beautiful" girl, Miller works from the assumption that such a combination carries certain imperatives; in this way, he sexualizes both characters. Abigail is not impervious to the currents running between her and Proctor. When he barges into the upstairs bedroom at Parris's home, she stands "as though on tiptoe, absorbing his presence, wide-eyed" and her first remark to him is "Gah! I'd almost forgot how strong you are, John Proctor" (239). Mercy has departed, "strangely titillated," and it's clear that both girls find something compelling about him. Abigail asks John for "a soft word," and she grasps his hand to assure him, "I am waitin' for you every night" (240). Her invitation is as frankly sexual as her vocabulary and experience will permit, and we know, though he does not, as yet, that she hopes to kill his wife in order to make room for her own hopes. Proctor cannot encounter Abigail without referring to her sexual potential and the sexual history of their relationship.

Abigail presses the encounter to a crisis and tears at the fabric of the community when she tearfully presents herself as an innocent led astray.

> I look for John Proctor that took me from my sleep and put knowledge in my heart! I never knew what pretense Salem was, I never knew the lying lessons I was taught by all these Christian women and their covenanted men! And now you bid me tear the light out of my eyes? I will not, I cannot! You loved me, John Proctor, and whatever sin it is, you love me yet. . . . *She rushes to him.* John, pity me, pity me! (241)

Miller orchestrates this moment, underscoring Abigail's tearful protest with the parishioners below singing a psalm that articulates the very "lying lessons" that the girl denounces. She is dangerous because she sees a truth that she is willing to speak. Putnam would separate the word from the action, just as Proctor would draw a veil over the past, but Abigail threatens to reveal the hypocrisy. Carnal knowledge becomes social knowledge and gives her power over others. Wendy Schissel takes Abigail's outburst as truthful, valid evidence that Proctor led Abigail astray; she argues that Proctor is the aggressor and she challenges the plausibility of Miller's premise, that a girl raised in repressed, sheltered circumstances could know how to seduce a man, a supposition that implies that such knowledge is inherent in all females (463–65). We could quibble over how much instruction any young person requires regarding sex, but we can accept Abigail's speech as truthful without necessarily attaching primary blame to either party; we can imagine two people crossing one careful boundary after another, each responding to the other's signals, testing each limit and moving on.[9] Nevertheless, in moral and everyday terms, Proctor is the adult and the employer, so he bore the responsibility of keeping the relationship under control. It seems clear that he knows that. Indeed, a central thread in Proctor's character is his keen sense of his own transgression; as Miller puts it, "He is a sinner, a sinner not only against the moral fashion of the time, but against his own vision of decent conduct" (239). He has done wrong by his own standards, and for that reason he hesitates to present himself to his wife or his community as a paragon. Certainly Abigail claims to find her newfound sexuality difficult to manage; she confesses to Hale (perhaps by way of tempting even that innocent cleric) that "sometimes I wake and find myself standing in the open doorway and not a stitch on my body," but she blames Tituba for working her magic on her (257). Abigail may very well be the victim of a seduction, even of rape, but now, as Betty lies whining on the bed, she is urging John to continue their relationship, to come to her at night and confirm her conviction that he loves her still. She plays the tactic that is, perhaps, most likely to win any man—she presents herself as willing and available.

What really happened in Proctor's barn? Who initiated the sexual encounter, and how willingly did each embrace the opportunity? For all Proctor's self-castigation, Miller suggests that he is the helpless victim of Abigail's charms, implicitly asking us to allow him an indulgence out of keeping with the strength of his character. If Proctor seduced Abigail and then rejected her, we can scarcely respect him; if he raped her, then we must condemn him and the play collapses. In any case, the episode seems to have paralyzed Proctor, for he condones his wife's decision to turn the girl out and thus suggest her guilt to the community while he evades public censure. Abigail appears as the evil one who has led the upright man astray.[10]

Abigail is, beneath it all, a survivor in a society that assigns her a subordinate role. She is a woman, a young woman, a young unmarried woman, and an orphan living off of her surly uncle's grudging generosity or her luck in finding a place as a servant. In the class structure of Salem, she finds herself inferior to all but such as Tituba, and as soon as Hale's interrogation moves beyond her ability to protect herself, she implicates the Barbados woman. At that point, Hale's eagerness to find someone trafficking with the Devil combines with Tituba's panicky need to exculpate herself to send the scene spinning out of control. When Abigail realizes that the terms of social interaction have changed, then in order to cut her losses and regain some measure of authority, she joins in the orgy of accusation. Abigail will do what she must, but she will not lose ground if there's any way to reinforce her position.

Notes

9. Schissel is skeptical, resisting the notion of woman as inevitable siren, but if young people needed instruction regarding their sexual capabilities, their elders would surely face less difficulty in maintaining their chastity than is typically the case. Possibly Schissel is drawing a distinction between seduction, with its implications of strategy and illicit behavior, and sanctioned sexual relationships, but surely it is not difficult to imagine a young girl acting on impulses and desires she does not fully understand, seeking proximity and contact, and further imagining a man of Proctor's age and health responding to her warmth, indulging himself with a hand on a shoulder, a quick embrace, or a chance to lift a girl down from a stepstool, and allowing the relationship to escalate.

10. In June 1953, Miller added a scene (now act 2, scene 2 in the Dramatists Play Service acting edition) that makes Abigail seem not only driven but actually insane. She and Proctor meet alone in the woods, late at night, and both dialogue and stage directions indicate that Abigail sees herself as victim, messenger of God, and Proctor's savior, acting with full belief that witches torment her and hypocrites surround her. She tells Proctor:

Why, you taught me goodness, therefore you are good. It were a fire you walked me through, and . . . you burned my ignorance away. As bare as some December tree I saw them all—walking like saints to church, running to feed the sick, and hypocrites in their hearts! And God gave me strength to call them liars, and God made men to listen to me, and by God I will scrub the world clean for the love of Him! Oh, John, I will make you such a wife when the world is white again! *She kisses his hand.* You will be amazed to see me every day, a light of heaven in your house . . .

This is a child whose transition into womanhood, with its awakening into passion and carnality, has hurled her into ecstatic madness.

CHRISTOPHER BIGSBY ON THE THEME OF BETRAYAL IN *THE CRUCIBLE*

If *The Crucible* is concerned with power, its source, its manipulation, its language, it is also concerned with betrayal. The historic John Proctor and Abigail Williams were distant in age. Miller narrowed the age gap and ignited a sexual flame, one with echoes in his own life. Marilyn, eleven years his junior, was a compelling presence in his mind, if not in his life, while his own marriage seemed increasingly cold, precisely John Proctor's dilemma in the play. As he observed in a typescript note in September 1976, he had strayed from his wife and was suffering from a sense of guilt. His decision to write *The Crucible* may have been socially motivated but he admitted, at least to himself in this private note, that it was also deeply implicated in his own life, in a sexuality to which he was drawn even as it left him in a state of confusion. But his real concern in introducing this element—for which, oddly, given her age, he thought he might have sanction, since Abigail Williams had been dismissed from the Proctor household—lay once again in his desire to link the private to the public. Proctor is a flawed man tempted to betray not only in private but in public when he agrees to sign his name to a falsehood. The play is in part to do with his recovery under pressure as he reinvests his name with an integrity he had come so close to surrendering. He dies to sustain his idea of himself and of a society in which such a death may redeem a sense of truth and justice momentarily laid aside out of fear.

In the first typescript of the play the sexual tension that motivates Abigail is introduced early. As she looks down at

Betty, seemingly unconscious on the bed after having spent the previous night dancing naked in the forest and conjuring spirits with Tituba, she is described as stretching the cloth of her gown against her body. She is, we are told, in the throes of a sensuous excitement and chants a verse in which she imagines herself in the arms of Proctor, who had been denied the marriage bed for seven months. Abigail has 'a sense for heat' and had felt him 'burning' in his loneliness. In that early draft Miller included a scene, subsequently dropped from most productions, in which Abigail and Proctor meet. Six months after the play opened, when Miller restaged it, he reinstated it. Proctor and Abigail come together the night before his wife is to appear in court. Abigail is dressed in a nightgown.

When Laurence Olivier directed a production in 1965 he hunted down the extra scene in a theatre magazine. In a letter to Miller dated 13 August 1964, he wrote: 'I was a wee bit disappointed when I read it because I suppose I had assumed that Abigail would have tried to seduce Proctor in this scene and only agree to clear Elizabeth [of a false charge of witchcraft] on this sort of bargain. Would there be anything in this note being struck in this scene?' He added, 'I have never thought that Abigail's line in Act I, "I know how you clutched my back . . .", really indicated the extent of the thing that had occurred, which we learn from Elizabeth, and later from Proctor, is a complete act of sex. Do you think you might strengthen Abigail's line into meaning all that it should mean?' Miller did not alter the line and Olivier decided against including the forest scene, explaining to Miller: 'You don't need it. It's nice when you read the play. You get an expanded view of it. But it destroyed that certain marching tempo that starts to get into that play to that place . . . thus scene stops the beat.'[57]

In the handwritten draft that preceded his first typed version, a draft partly set out in verse, Abigail confesses her desire, her passion being pitched against the cold judgement of Elizabeth Proctor who, at this early stage of the text, her husband half believes, may have set herself to destroy him.

In 1998, Miller saw evidence of a political conservatism rooted in a concern with sexuality that seemed all too familiar.

This time it was not a young woman called Abigail Williams at the centre of events but one called Monica Lewinsky (with whom he appeared on the television program *60 Minutes*, oddly admiring of someone he thought of as a twentieth-century courtesan). In the right-wing attacks on President Clinton he heard echoes of the hatred that seemed to him to recall the Salem ministers attacking the Devil while revelling, lubriciously, in a suddenly exposed sexuality. Exposure had a double significance. Suddenly things could be spoken aloud that had previously been sublimated, denied. The fascination with witchcraft, and the laying-out of the details of sexual encounter, both betokened a fear of women and the displacement on to them of male desire, otherwise cloaked in the guise of moral concern. The sanctimonious denunciation, it seemed to him, whether in Puritan New England or in the guise of a twentieth-century special prosecutor, barely concealed not only personal ambition but something more radical in the human sensibility. Monica Lewinsky and Abigail would have recognized one another; but so, too, he thought, would Kenneth Starr and the Puritan judges come together to explore the details of a supposed depravity. There was, in short, a parallel in the sexual element. . . . Witch-hunts are always spooked by women's horrifying sexuality awakened by the superstud Devil. . . . In Salem, witch-hunting ministers had the solemn duty to examine women's bodies for signs of 'the Devil's Marks.' . . . I thought of this wonderfully holy exercise when Congress was pawing through Kenneth Starr's fiercely exact report on the President's intimate meetings with Monica Lewinsky.

Hatred for Clinton, it seemed to him, amounted to a 'hellish fear of him as unclean'.[58] Sex, however, was to be only one element in a play in which betrayal broadened out until it became a civic and, indeed, religious duty. Miller was concerned to underscore the moral and social implications of betrayals presented as duty, as brother is set to spy on brother while the fields go untended. At the same time, he was aware that to deny witchcraft was to invite the charge of trying to conceal the conspiracy and discredit those who alone claimed to be able to save the community. The parallel with HUAC was too compelling to be ignored. The accuser becomes an agent of the state, his or her accusation assuming a presumptive right. Here was a tragedy, it seemed to him, precisely of Greek proportions, in which the fate of the state was invested in the drama of a man who embraces his own fate in order to sustain a principle which he had come so close to abrogating. John Proctor rediscovers his integrity and in doing so potentially redeems his society. Justice is not done, but the principle of justice is upheld.

In 2002, Miller looked back to the 1950s: 'We lived in a time,' he observed, 'distorted by obligatory and defensive patriotism, an atmosphere unimaginable anymore.'[59] It was a time when the urgencies of the moment seemed to justify the laying aside of the very values that were to have sustained the society, just as they had in Puritan New England. But the processes that he identifies were not unique to those moments, nor, it would turn out, unimaginable.

Notes

57. Letter from Laurence Olivier in Miller's private papers.

58. Arthur Miller, 'Salem Revisited', *New York Times*, 15 October 1998.

59. Arthur Miller, 'Steinbeck', in *John Steinbeck: A Centennial Tribute*, ed. Stephen K. George (Westport, 2002), p. 64.

Works by Arthur Miller

Situation Normal, 1944.

Focus, 1945.

All My Sons, 1947.

Death of a Salesman: Certain Private Conversations in Two Acts and a Requiem, 1949.

An Enemy of the People by Henrik Ibsen (adaptor), 1951.

The Crucible, 1953.

A View from the Bridge (with A Memory of Two Mondays): Two One-Act Plays, 1955.

Collected Plays, two volumes, 1957, 1981.

The Misfits, 1961.

Jane's Blanket, 1963.

After the Fall, 1964.

Incident at Vichy, 1965.

I Don't Need You Any More: Stories (as *The Misfits and Other Stories*), 1967, 1987.

The Price, 1968.

In Russia (with Inge Morath), 1969.

The Portable Arthur Miller, ed. Harold Clurman, 1971, ed. Christopher Bigsby, 1995.

The Creation of the World and Other Business, 1973.

In the Country (with Inge Morath), 1977.

The Theater Essays of Arthur Miller, ed. Robert A. Martin, 1978.

Chinese Encounter (with Inge Morath), 1979.

Eight Plays, 1981.

Playing for Time: A Screenplay, 1981.

The American Clock, 1982.

Elegy for a Lady, 1982.

Some Kind of Love Story, 1983.

Salesman *in Beijing*, 1984.

The Archbishop's Ceiling, 1984.

Two-Way Mirror: A Double Bill (*Elegy for a Lady* and *Some Kind of Love Story*), 1984.

Up from Paradise, 1984.

Playing for Time: A Full-Length Play, 1985.

Danger: Memory! (*I Can't Remember Anything* and *Clara*), 1986.

Timebends: A Life, 1987.

Conversations with Arthur Miller, ed. Matthew C. Roudané, 1987.

Plays: One, 1988.

Plays: Two, 1988.

The Archbishop's Ceiling; The American Clock, 1988.

The Golden Years and The Man Who Had All the Luck, 1989.

Early Plays, 1989.

On Censorship and Laughter, 1990.

Plays: Three, 1990.

Everybody Wins: A Screenplay, 1990.

The Last Yankee (one-scene version), 1991; (two-scene version), 1993.

The Ride down Mt. Morgan, 1991.

Homely Girl, A Life (with Louise Bourgeois), two volumes, 1992.

Arthur Miller in Conversation, ed. Steven R. Centola, 1993.

Broken Glass, 1994.

The Last Yankee: with a New Essay about Theatre Language and Broken Glass, 1994.

Plays: Four, 1994.

Homely Girl, A Life and Other Stories, 1995.

The Theater Essays of Arthur Miller (revised and expanded), eds. Robert A. Martin and Steven R. Centola, 1996.

Mr. Peter's Connections, 1998.

Echoes Down the Corridor: Collected Essays, 1944–2000, 2000.

On Politics and the Art of Acting, 2001.

Resurrection Blues, 2002.

Bhatia, Santosh K. *Arthur Miller: Social Drama as Tragedy*. New Delhi: Arnold-Heinemann Publishers, 1985.

An Indian scholar, Bhatia takes on the concept of tragedy in both its Greek and Shakespearean forms. He begins by listing the five essential elements of tragedy—conflict, suffering, tragic irony, awakening, and metaphysical considerations. In his study of major Miller plays—*All My Sons*, *Death of a Salesman*, *The Crucible*, *A View from the Bridge*, and *The Price*—he focuses on the way they involve social issues while conforming to the traditional characteristics of tragedy.

Bigsby, Christopher. *Arthur Miller: 1915–1962*. Cambridge, Mass: Harvard University Press, 2009.

Bigsby has published other works on Arthur Miller, but this volume is his most ambitious despite its stated focus on the first half of Miller's life. The author is writing as much as a historian as he is a literary critic: He believes Miller's developing relationship with his country—troubled, triumphant, painful, and reverent—reveals the important enduring truths about U.S. history, politics, and culture. Bigsby gives a detailed picture of Miller's early influences in his years in Harlem and Brooklyn and his college years at the University of Michigan. In addition to chapters on five of his most important plays, there is a chapter each devoted to his marriages to Marilyn Monroe and Inge Morath and one on his harassment by Joseph McCarthy and the infamous House on Un-American Activities Committee.

Brater, Enoch. *Arthur Miller: A Playwright's Life and Works*. London: Thames & Hudson, Ltd., 2005.

This volume is distinguished by the inclusion of 70 black-and-white photographs (some full page) from various stage productions of his work, his personal life, and marriages.

———, ed. *Arthur Miller's America: Theater & Culture in a Time of Change*. Ann Arbor: The University of Michigan Press, 2005.

The idea for this volume was generated at a symposium at the University of Michigan organized to honor Arthur Miller in his 85th year. The participants invited to speak—friends, students, actors, colleagues, and literary critics—were inspired to reformulate their presentations and discussions that followed in such a way as to make them available to a wider public audience and readership. Twenty chapters—covering most of the proceedings—offer new insights into Miller's life, plays, and his work's impact on recent American history.

Martine, James J., ed. *Critical Essays on Arthur Miller*. Boston: G. K. Hall & Co., 1979.

This group of essays is organized around the plays with a chapter on each with commentary by one or more contributors. The book concludes with an interview of Miller by the editor and some general commentary on Miller's short stories, cultural roots, and influence.

Mason, Jeffrey D. *Stone Tower: The Political Theater of Arthur Miller*. Ann Arbor: The University of Michigan Press, 2008.

Mason introduces his book with an explanation of the origins and significance of its title. The image of a "blasted stone tower" appears prominently on the stage of Miller's play *After the Fall*. It is described as standing on the site of a German concentration camp and signifies oppressive power, force, allegiance, conflict, and destruction. Mason explains that he chose this symbol to emphasize those central concerns and experiences in Miller's politically active life. Many critics have been appropriately preoccupied with the social issues dramatized in the plays, but Mason makes the important distinction between social and political issues, viewing Miller as an artist who—among other things—was concerned with and successful at raising awareness of the serious political trends of the times.

Miller, Arthur. *Timebends: A Life*. New York: Grove Press, 1987.

This memoir is Miller's famous effort to describe his life and works, an autobiography with history and social/political commentary. Published in 1987, this animated and accessible work covers only part of his life. Of particular value are Miller's reports on how he imagined and then prepared for writing his plays. For example, he gives an intimate account of his changing relationship with director Elia Kazan and his wife, Molly, before, during, and after the HUAC hearings and the phenomenon known as blacklisting.

Weales, Gerald, ed. *Arthur Miller: "The Crucible."* New York: Penguin, 1996.

This study from the Viking Critical Library is an excellent introduction to *The Crucible*. It includes early reviews, essays and texts on the historical context, and general commentary on the play's themes and influences. Although the book is not a biography, it includes a section that discusses Miller's life as it intersected with the issues raised in the play.

# Contributors

Harold Bloom is Sterling Professor of the Humanities at Yale University. Educated at Cornell and Yale universities, he is the author of more than 30 books, including *Shelley's Mythmaking* (1959), *The Visionary Company* (1961), *Blake's Apocalypse* (1963), *Yeats* (1970), *The Anxiety of Influence* (1973), *A Map of Misreading* (1975), *Kabbalah and Criticism* (1975), *Agon: Toward a Theory of Revisionism* (1982), *The American Religion* (1992), *The Western Canon* (1994), *Omens of Millennium: The Gnosis of Angels, Dreams, and Resurrection* (1996), *Shakespeare: The Invention of the Human* (1998), *How to Read and Why* (2000), *Genius: A Mosaic of One Hundred Exemplary Creative Minds* (2002), *Hamlet: Poem Unlimited* (2003), *Where Shall Wisdom Be Found?* (2004), and *Jesus and Yahweh: The Names Divine* (2005). In addition, he is the author of hundreds of articles, reviews, and editorial introductions. In 1999, Professor Bloom received the American Academy of Arts and Letters' Gold Medal for Criticism. He has also received the International Prize of Catalonia, the Alfonso Reyes Prize of Mexico, and the Hans Christian Andersen Bicentennial Prize of Denmark.

John Hale is both a historical figure and a character in *The Crucible*. The historical Hale was a minister and man of learning in the Salem Puritan community. He was called to the Salem trials to weigh the evidence as an objective outsider. In 1702, his examination of these trials was published. It described his movement from believing in the reality of "agents of the Devil" to questioning trial tactics, authenticity, and outcomes. In the play he is summoned as an expert in witchcraft; his interrogation of Tituba, in particular, follows the historical transcript Miller found in the record at the Salem courthouse.

Robert A. Martin is the editor of *The Theater Essays of Arthur Miller* (1977) and *Critical Essays on Tennessee Williams* (1997). He taught in the department of English at the University of Michigan at Ann Arbor.

Santosh K. Bhatia is associated with Guru Nanak Dev University in India.

Karen Bovard is employed by the Connecticut Independent School system where she teaches high school theater, English, and history. She is the former artistic director of the Oddfellows Playhouse Youth Theater and current director of the Creative Arts Program at Watkinson School in Hartford, Connecticut. Her essays have been published in *Teaching Tolerance*, *Theater Journal*, and *Stage of the Art*.

Enoch Brater teaches in the English and theater department at the University of Michigan in Ann Arbor. In addition to his work on Arthur Miller, he has published three books on Samuel Beckett: *The Essential Samuel Beckett*, *The Drama in the Text: Beckett's Late Fiction*, and *Beyond Minimalism: Beckett's Late Style in the Theater*.

Steven R. Centola was the founder of the Arthur Miller Society and a renowned Arthur Miller scholar during his professional life. He taught English at Millersville University in Pennsylvania. Among his many publications are *The Achievement of Arthur Miller: New Essays* and two books written in collaboration with Miller: *The Theater Essays of Arthur Miller* and *Echoes Down the Corridor: Collected Essays 1944–2000*.

D. Quentin Miller teaches in the department of English at Suffolk University. In addition to his work on Miller, he has contributed an essay on John Updike to *The Cambridge Companion to John Updike* (2006) and an essay on James Baldwin, "Reviewing James Baldwin: Things Not Seen" to the *African American Review* (Winter 2001).

Jeffrey D. Mason was head of the department of theater arts at the University of Oregon and, in 2006, became dean of the College of Arts and Letters at Sacramento State College. He has played many roles onstage including Danforth in *The Crucible*.

Christopher Bigsby is a professor of American studies at the University of East Anglia in Norwich, England. He is also the director of the Arthur Miller Center for American Studies. Bigsby is considered one of the world's most prominent analysts of the theater and one of the authoritative writers about Arthur Miller. In addition to his voluminous 2009 study of Miller, he is the author of *Remembering Arthur Miller* (2005) and *Arthur Miller & Company* (1990).

Acknowledgments

John Hale, "How Persons Guilty of that Crime may be Convicted: And the means used for their Discovery Discussed, both Negatively and Affirmatively, according to Scripture and Experience." From *A Modest Enquiry into the Nature of Witchcraft*, Boston, 1702. Reprinted in *Arthur Miller: "The Crucible," Text and Criticism*, edited by Gerald Weales, pp. 384–87. New York and Middlesex, England: Penguin Books Ltd. Copyright © 1971, The Viking Press.

Robert A. Martin, "Arthur Miller's The Crucible: Background and Sources." From *Modern Drama* 20 (1977): 279–92. Copyright © 1977 *Modern Drama*, the Graduate Centre for the Study of Drama at the University of Toronto. Reprinted by permission of University of Toronto Press Incorporated (www.utpjournals.com).

Santosh K. Bhatia, "The Crucible." From *Arthur Miller: Social Drama as Tragedy*, pp. 63–67, 69–70. New Delhi: Arnold-Heinemann Publishers. Copyright © 1985, Santosh K. Bhatia.

Arthur Miller, excerpt from *Timebends: A Life*, pp. 330–31, 335–36, 337, 338, 339. Published by Grove Press. Copyright © 1987, 1995 by Arthur Miller, used electronically with permission of The Wylie Agency LLC.

Karen Bovard, from "Witch-Hunting, Thwarted Desire, and Girl Power: Arthur Miller's *The Crucible* (1953)," pp. 82–84. From *Women in Literature: Reading Through the Lens of Gender*, edited by Jerilyn Fisher and Ellen S. Silber. Published by Greenwood Press. Copyright © 2003 by Jerilyn Fisher and Ellen S. Silber. Reproduced with permission of ABC-CLIO, LLC.

Enoch Brater, from *Arthur Miller: A Playwright's Life and Works*, pp. 53–66. Copyright © 2005 Thames & Hudson

Index

Characters in literary works are indexed by first name (if any), followed by the name of the work in parentheses

DRAMA
CRITICISMS